THE ART OF
Numerology

THE ART OF
Numerology

A practical guide to uncover your destiny

Edited by
ANNA SOUTHGATE

STERLING ETHOS
New York

STERLING ETHOS
New York

An Imprint of Sterling Publishing Co., Inc.
1166 Avenue of the Americas
New York, NY 10036

ISBN 978-1-4549-2144-8

For information about custom editions, special sales,
and premium and corporate purchases, please contact
Sterling Special Sales at 800-805-5489 or
specialsales@sterlingpublishing.com.

Manufactured in China

2 4 6 8 10 9 7 5 3 1

www.sterlingpublishing.com

CONTENTS

INTRODUCTION

From the moment you are born, you are allocated numbers that are important to you: your date of birth, passport number, house number, Social Security number, bank account number, and car license number, to name but a few. Should you ever be convicted of a felony, you'll be reduced to the most basic component—the prisoner number. In this book, you will learn a great deal about the magic of numbers, including their symbolic significance, the nature of their vibrations, their lore, and their secret meanings.

Numerology is one of the oldest analytical techniques in the world, and can be traced back to the Babylonians. The Ancient Egyptians had their own numerology system, with occult powers attributed to each number; they used numerology as a means of understanding human psychology. Judaism holds what is probably the greatest key to the lore of numerology through the Kabbalah, a secret mystical text containing the philosophical science of numbers. In the 13th century, scholars of the Kabbalah developed the Gematria, a method of interpreting the Bible whereby inferences were drawn from the numerical value of the letters of the Hebrew alphabet. Using this method, Kabbalist scholars would search for hidden meanings in the text of the Old Testament.

THE CHRISTIAN TRADITION

Numbers have long had great symbolic spiritual significance in the Christian tradition. In the Middle Ages, numbers and geometry found their way into nearly every aspect of cathedral design, from the number of pillars to the layout of the façade. Number symbolism also features heavily in Christian theology. Well-known

A numerical calculation table, based upon the work of medieval Kabbalist Johannes Reuchlin, using gematric principles to equate Hebrew letters (right-hand column) with numbers (1838).

examples include the two natures of Christ (human and divine), the Trinity, the four points of the Cross, the triple six (the number of the beast or the antichrist), the seven virtues and vices, the nine choirs of angels, and the twelve Apostles or disciples. The number thirteen, commonly thought of as the number of bad luck, symbolizes faithlessness and betrayal—the number of Apostles plus Judas.

PYTHAGORAS

There is no doubt that the Greek philosopher and mathematician Pythagoras (c. 580–500 BC) is the father of Western

▲ Pythagoras, at the center of this 16th-century fresco, created the system for calculating personal numbers that is most popular today.

numerology in the form that we know it today. Pythagoras believed that the world is built upon the power of numbers. In his words, "everything is numbers and to know numbers is to know thyself." According to Pythagorean theory, everything in the universe is composed of mathematical patterns, and thus all things can be expressed in numbers that

correspond to universal vibrations. In this way, Pythagoras believed, numbers are the keys that can unlock the secrets of the universe and nature. It was Pythagoras who laid down the basic tenets of Western numerology, which operates by reducing compound numbers down to the nine primary numbers, each of which is assigned a particular meaning and symbolism. According to this methodology, all names and birth dates can be reduced to numbers in order to determine the personalities and destinies of individuals.

△ John Dee Performing an Experiment Before Queen Elizabeth I by Henry Gillard Glindoni.

THE MIDDLE AGES

In medieval times, numerology was known as arithomancy or numeromancy, and was used for predicting the future. It was also used widely in conjunction with astrology and divination. One method of divination involved using Tablets of Fate (see pages 42–49), upon which numbers were cast in order to divine the possible answers to certain questions that an individual wanted answered. One of the most well-known numerologists during these times was Dr. John Dee. Dr. Dee was the official court magician of Queen Elizabeth I of England, and she relied heavily upon his divinatory powers. He was even asked to work out the most auspicious date for her coronation.

NUMEROLOGY TODAY

Because Pythagoras left only fragmented details of his system of numerology, there are many differences in numerological interpretation today. For the purposes of this book, we have chosen to interpret the meanings as follows: our Birth Number can tell us about our basic character and Life Path; our Full Name Number lets us know how we present ourselves to others and how they see us; and our Known Name Number illuminates for us our inner personality. Together, these three numbers can be expressed as a three-digit number, such as 4–5–7 or 9–3–1. There are 729 possible combinations of these three numbers. (A reading for each combination is provided on pages 50–141.)

WHY NUMEROLOGY WORKS

One of the basic tenets of Western numerology is that everything in the world is constantly vibrating with energy. Numbers are viewed as symbols of the constant cycle of energy, and are thought to reveal the patterns of life itself. Each number has its own unique vibrations, and each represents specific powers and opportunities. According to numerology, the numbers that are ascribed to each individual (particularly through their birth date and name) form a template for the energy in that person's life. Through awareness of the powers and principles of numerology, each individual can discover how to change the energy surrounding his or her life to achieve a harmonious vibration and reach his or her maximum potential.

Once we understand the basic significance of numbers, we can begin to apply their meanings to everyday situations. Numerology can help us in many facets of our lives. It can tell us which colors are best suited to our home and wardrobe, and which days and years will be lucky for us. It can also tell us how we can change our names to bring luck and fortune into our lives, and what we should look for in the personal numbers of our business partners, friends, and lovers. We can even use numerology to see into the future.

Like scrying, numerology can be used to help you see what the future might hold in store for you.

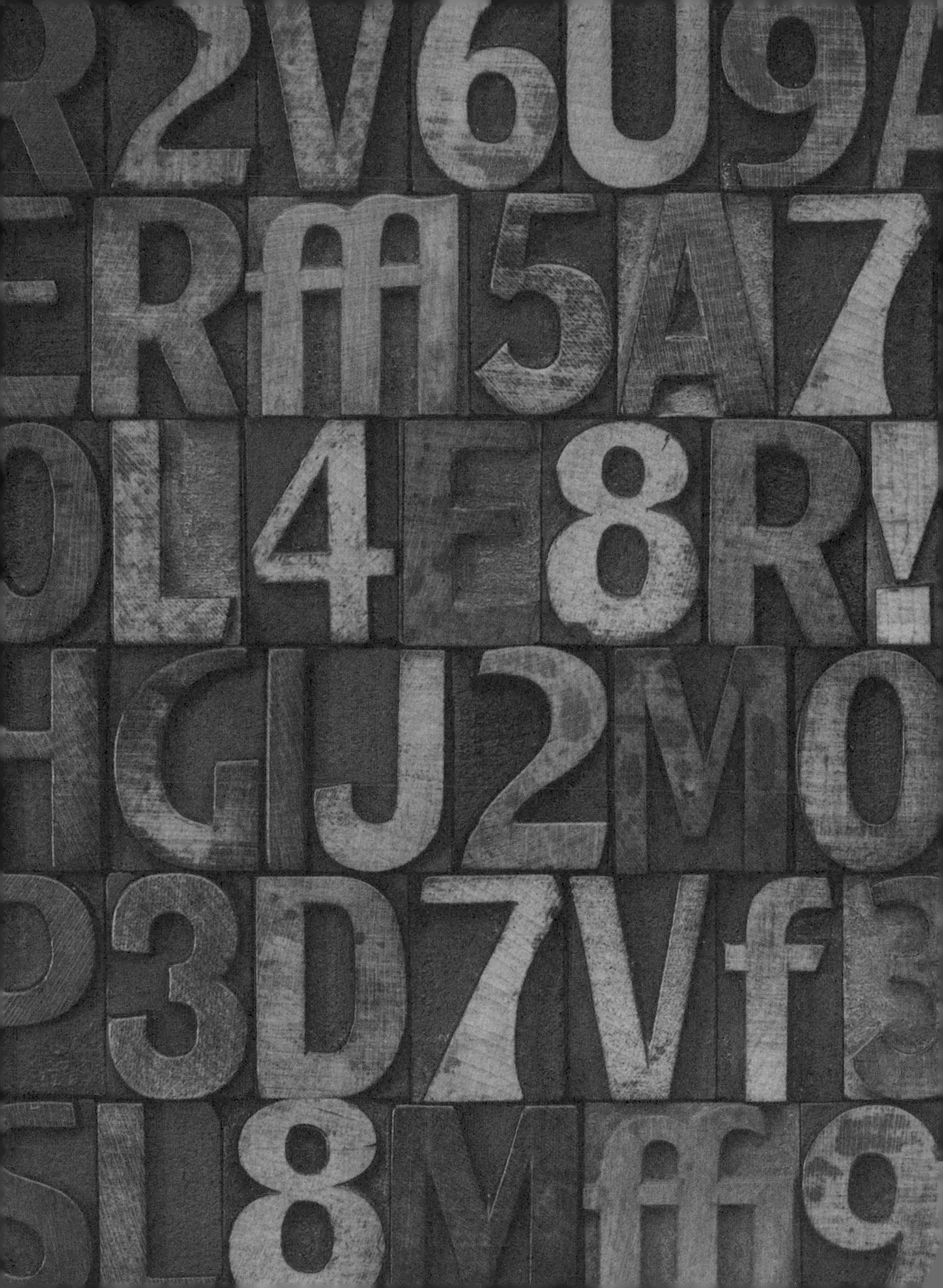

PART 1

PRINCIPLES OF NUMEROLOGY

In the Western system of numerology, which is based on the Pythagorean method, each letter of the alphabet is given a number between 1 and 9. Each of the nine numbers has its own special symbolism and meaning. As you progress through the book and learn how to figure out your personal numbers, you will need to refer back to the explanation of the nine numbers that follows.

PRIMARY NUMBERS

THE MEANING OF THE NUMBERS
Below is an at-a-glance guide to the meaning of the nine primary numbers.

	1	Strong, ambitious, innovative, active, creative
	2	Artistic, gentle, thoughtful, inventive, charming, intuitive
	3	Energetic, disciplined, talented, successful, independent, controlling
	4	Steady, practical, enduring, rebellious, unconventional, isolated
	5	Lively, pleasure-seeking, impulsive, quick-tempered, entrepreneurial
	6	Reliable, trustworthy, loving, caring, resolute, communicative
	7	Spiritual, introverted, psychic, lucky, restless, intuitive
	8	Successful, obstinate, individual, intense, difficult, rebellious
	9	Active, determined, quarrelsome, courageous, dangerous

NUMEROLOGY NAME: MONAD

1		
	DAY	Sunday
	COLOR	Red
	CAREERS	Design, inventing, teaching, writing
	KEY ATTRIBUTES	Active, resolute, tenacious, confident
	NEGATIVE ASPECTS	Intolerant, critical, arrogant
	SOCIAL ASPECTS	Quiet, independent

Number 1 represents the Sun. It is the number of strength, individuality, and creativity. People with this number will never lack confidence or need reassuring. They are straightforward, bright, and honest people who love being out in the world and enjoy moving forward in life. They are natural leaders and innovators, and have a great need to be in the limelight. In its positive aspect, the number 1 is honest and upright; in its negative aspect, it is domineering and bossy. It is the sign of the saint and the tyrant, the saviour and the dictator. Number 1 people have endless enthusiasm and energy, and others who are less outgoing may find them intimidating and exhausting. Number 1 people can often, however, feel isolated and lonely. They strive to please others, but frequently fail owing to their belief that they are always right. Thus, their life lesson is to learn diplomacy.

▶ The Sun tarot card from the late 15th-century Italian deck known as the Charles VI or Gringonneur tarot.

NUMEROLOGY NAME: DUAD

2		
	DAY	Monday
	COLOR	Orange
	CAREERS	Nursing, any area of hospitality, art, therapy
	KEY ATTRIBUTES	Diplomatic, creative, intuitive, emotional
	NEGATIVE ASPECTS	Passive, deceitful, depressive
	SOCIAL ASPECTS	Outgoing, friendly, supportive

▲ **Diana the Huntress** by Guillaume Seignac, 19th century. The Roman lunar goddess is associated with emotions.

Number 2 represents the Moon. It is the number of creativity, femininity, and gentleness. The typical number 2 person is more concerned with emotions than action. They are usually charming, sensitive, and intuitive. They are also changeable, and can adapt to virtually any situation. They get along very well with other people, and are caring and supportive. Number 2 people are typically diplomatic and like a peaceful life. This can lead to problems, however, as they prefer to avoid taking responsibility or making decisions. They are romantic and idealistic—sometimes overly so—and have a clear vision of what life should be like. Number 2 people have problems with self-confidence at times, however, and can be reluctant to see ideas through.

Number 3 represents the family and the planet Jupiter. It is also the number of the Trinity. In ancient times, it was regarded as the perfect number, as it represents time, matter, and space; length, breadth, and depth; and solid, liquid, and gas. It was also linked to the triangle, which is the symbol of logic, intellect, and reason. Three is also the number of success and completion. Number 3 people know how to see projects through, always meet their deadlines, and are energetic and disciplined. They are independent and like to work hard, achieving success by overcoming odds and adversity. They enjoy a challenge, and will often seek out difficult situations so that they can be seen as trouble-shooters. They are also talkative and are very sure of themselves. Those with this number are freedom-loving and strong, organized and enthusiastic, and optimistic and tenacious. They can, at times, be slightly indifferent to the feelings of others, and tend to brush aside opinions somewhat briskly.

▲ Like the White Rabbit from **Alice's Adventures in Wonderland**, number 3 people value punctuality.

NUMEROLOGY NAME: TERN

3		
	DAY	Tuesday
	COLOR	Yellow
	CAREERS	Entrepreneurship, law, business, sales, communications
	KEY ATTRIBUTES	Energetic, successful, talented, punctual
	NEGATIVE ASPECTS	Proud, controlling, interfering
	SOCIAL ASPECTS	Outgoing, talkative, gregarious

NUMEROLOGY NAME: QUATERNION

4

DAY	Wednesday
COLOR	Green
CAREERS	Mathematics, architecture, engineering
KEY ATTRIBUTES	Dependable, trustworthy, endurance, stamina
NEGATIVE ASPECTS	Unemotional, impatient, reckless
SOCIAL ASPECTS	Reclusive, unconventional

Number 4 represents the planet Uranus as well as the four seasons, the points of the compass, and the four elements. It is the number of reliability and steadfastness. Those with this number are practical and down-to-earth. In fact, earth is the best word to describe the number 4. Number 4 people are earthy in humor and life, robust and strong, and enduring and plucky. They enjoy the good things in life in abundance, and like to indulge themselves. Hedonistic by nature, they enjoy experiences and sensations, and have little interest in accumulating material possessions. Although number 4 people can be bombastic and opinionated, they are always enthusiastic and full of life. They enjoy their own company, and don't suffer fools easily. The typical number 4 person may only have a few close friends rather than a lot of casual acquaintances and may be considered introverted. Number 4 people have great loyalty to both people and ideas. They are adept at processing abstract thoughts and turning them into logical, sensible opinions.

A 16th-century woodcut of the four humors in relation to the four elements and the signs of the zodiac.

NUMEROLOGY NAME: QUINCUNX

5		
	DAY	Thursday
	COLOR	Blue
	CAREERS	Public relations, advertising, acting, journalism, management
	KEY ATTRIBUTES	Sensuous, changeable, impulsive
	NEGATIVE ASPECTS	Nervous, highly strung, easily bored
	SOCIAL ASPECTS	Fun-loving, sociable, loquacious

Number 5 represents the planet Mercury. It is the number of the senses and of social graces. People with this number are witty and charming, and are full of enthusiasm and life. Others find them good company and like being around them, as they are able to cheer everyone up by their presence alone. Change is a key word for number 5 people. They often experience a great deal of upheaval in their lives, all of which they adapt to easily and readily. They tend to recover quickly from adversity and bounce back easily from setbacks. Number 5 people are very good with words, and find it easy to learn languages. They like to exercise their intellectual capacity, and find puzzles and games challenging and enticing. Some number 5 people have quick tempers, however, and can be highly strung. They don't like being stuck in a rut, and will go downhill quickly if caught in one.

Miniature illumination of the Hindu god Krishna playing chess with a woman. Many number 5 people like to exercise their minds with games and puzzles.

NUMEROLOGY NAME: HEXAD

6

DAY	Friday
COLOR	Indigo
CAREERS	Fashion, theater, charity work, beauty, modeling, music
KEY ATTRIBUTES	Romantic, idealistic, sensual
NEGATIVE ASPECTS	Passive, deceitful, depressive
SOCIAL ASPECTS	Friendly, outgoing, sociable

▲ **Venus Consoling Cupid,** c. 1802. Many number 6 people are hopeless romantics, and fall desperately in love quickly and easily. They also tend to be sensuous souls who appreciate beauty.

Number 6 represents the planet Venus. It is the number of harmony, beauty, balance, and perfection. Those with this number are reliable and trustworthy, romantic and sensual, and attractive and cheerful. They are very home-based, and like organizing and being in charge of a family, but their secret love is performing for others— acting or singing is often in their bones. They are also softhearted and loving, and consider it their duty to care for underdogs and stray animals. Most number 6 people like working for charities and enjoy helping others less fortunate than themselves, especially those in need of physical assistance. They are very idealistic and rarely practical, especially about the causes of poverty or suffering. These people have an air of martyrdom about them, and expect everything to be alright without considering the practicalities of their charitable endeavors. They typically need to learn how to stand up for themselves more.

Number 7 represents the planet Neptune. It is the number of travel and the occult. Those with this number are intuitive and psychic, sensitive and spiritual, and pensive and philosophical. They may well exert considerable influence upon those around them by sheer force of personality without even realizing it. Number 7 people may seem a little cold and unemotional on the outside, but in reality nothing could be further from the truth—in fact, there is a great deal of turmoil and many intense feelings churning around inside of them. They are simply shy, and find it a bit hard to open up. Number 7 people invariably have others coming to them for advice and help, although they may well resent the intrusions into their time and space. Their opinions, no matter how reluctantly given, are always valued, and they are seen by others as mentally superior.

▲ A 16th-century alchemist. Mysticism and the occult are two of the typical number 7 person's favorite subjects.

NUMEROLOGY NAME: SEPTENARY

7	DAY	Saturday
	COLOR	Violet
	CAREERS	Healing, counselling, therapy, clairvoyance, astrology, music
	KEY ATTRIBUTES	Intuitive, intellectual, psychic, unique
	NEGATIVE ASPECTS	Introverted, insensitive, unsettled
	SOCIAL ASPECTS	Aloof, reserved

Saturn riding the zodiac sign Capricorn, from a 16th-century Turkish treatise on astrology.

Number 8 represents the planet Saturn. It is the number of willpower and individuality, intensity and depth, and lessons and karmic duty. Those with this number may well be rebellious and unconventional, but these characteristics only drive them forward to accumulate great material success and wealth. They have an enormous amount of willpower, as well as individuality and strength of character. They know what needs to be done, and are usually very focused and goal-oriented. Number 8 people have great organizational abilities, and are naturally respected and looked up to. They are born leaders, and work well in a team—especially if they are in charge of it. They can push those under their command extremely hard, setting very high standards and producing spectacular results. Number 8 people are known for their courage, and they are not frightened to speak their minds—even if it makes them unpopular or controversial.

NUMEROLOGY NAME: OCTAD

8		
	DAY	Sunday
	COLOR	Dark red, crimson, purple, black
	CAREERS	The military, business, finance, politics, law, entrepreneurship
	KEY ATTRIBUTES	Original, intense, imaginative, decisive
	NEGATIVE ASPECTS	Domineering, blunt, tactless
	SOCIAL ASPECTS	Leading, organizing, sociable

NUMEROLOGY NAME: NONES

<table>
<tr><td rowspan="7" style="font-size:huge">9</td></tr>
<tr><td>DAY</td><td>Monday</td></tr>
<tr><td>COLOR</td><td>White, pink</td></tr>
<tr><td>CAREERS</td><td>Music, hypnotism, exploration, travel, clairvoyance, healing, writing</td></tr>
<tr><td>KEY ATTRIBUTES</td><td>Quirky, active, courageous, emotional</td></tr>
<tr><td>NEGATIVE ASPECTS</td><td>Dreamy, unrealistic, clinging, addictive</td></tr>
<tr><td>SOCIAL ASPECTS</td><td>Companionable, intense, wacky</td></tr>
</table>

Number 9 represents the planet Mars. It is the number of expression, both in the arts and in speech. Number 9 people have a great need to explore the depths of the human soul and express the universal poetry found there. They are creative, imaginative, sensitive, and intuitive people. They are also fighters and champions of the underdog. They like to take on causes—some of which may be unrealistic—and to aim for the goals that others would think unobtainable. People with this number have a great love of the exotic, strange, and freakish, and they may be attracted to people with odd quirks of personality and character. They can be very intense, and like to pick quarrels at times. These people are also active, and enjoy the thrill of danger and excitement. Number 9 people have problems at times with relationships, and tend to have trouble finding partners who will understand their need to express virtually everything they feel, see, and do.

▲ A stage hypnotist mesmerizing a blindfolded woman. Number 9 people are expressive and intuitive.

SECONDARY NUMBERS

The numbers 1 through 9 are the essential numbers in numerology. In order to do a proper numerological reading, each of the three personal numbers must be broken down to a single-digit number. There are, however, some double-digit numbers that may appear during the calculation process (see pages 24–29) that are also important. These are called secondary numbers, and they have their own special meaning and significance. Make a note of these, and use them to flesh out the reading from the final single-digit number. The secondary numbers and their meanings are set out here.

THE MEANING OF THE NUMBERS

Below are the secondary numbers and their interpretations. The most powerful secondary numbers are 11, 12, 13, 22, and 40.

10	Attainment	17	Creativity, imagination
11	Special mystical awareness	18	Strength, achievement
12	Completeness	19	Misfortune, self-destruction
13	Magic and mystery	20	Steadying influence
14	Overcoming obstacles, stoicism	21	Freedom, independence
		22	Achievement, success
15	Obstinacy, recklessness	40	Change, questioning
16	Excessive confidence		

If you work out your Birth Number, Known Name Number, or Full Name Number (see pages 24–29), and it comes out as a double-digit number, you may not want to reduce it down to a single-digit number so quickly. If the two-digit number is a number between 10 and 22, or the number 40, it is significant in its own right, and can add to the information obtained from your single-digit personal number. For instance, suppose your known name is Jon, which adds up to 12 (1 + 6 + 5). If you add the 1 and 2 together, reducing the number to a single digit, then Jon has a Known Name Number of 3, which means that he is energetic, disciplined, talented, successful, independent, and controlling. He is also a 12 as a secondary number, which signifies completeness. Modify any of Jon's key characteristics with the word "complete" and his reading becomes more detailed. We now know that Jon is talented, with the ability to complete projects. He is energetic, and his completeness gives him stamina. He is independent and successful, and feels a sense of wholeness in his life—in other words, his independence and success make him feel fulfilled.

◀ The serpent Ouroboros, an ancient symbol of primordial unity, cyclic renewal, and completeness. Use secondary numbers for a more complete numerology reading.

BIRTH NUMBER

The date, time, and place of birth are equally important for divining purposes in numerology. For our purposes, we will concentrate on the birth date number, also known as the Life Path number, which represents and reflects a person's inner potential. If you feel lost or indecisive, your Birth Number can help set you on the right path. Your Birth Number also shows your inherent talents and capabilities.

To figure out your Birth Number, add together the day, month, and year in which you were born, separating all the digits out. For example, if your birthday were November 21, 1964, you would add it up the following way:

$$1 + 1 + 2 + 1 + 1 + 9 + 6 + 4 = 25$$

You would then reduce the number 25 down to a single-digit number:

$$2 + 5 = 7$$

Thus, your Birth Number would be 7. This number represents the character you were born with: your instincts, your karmic duty and lessons, your genetic makeup, your traits and flaws, and your life direction. If your Birth Number is 7, you are spiritual, sensitive, and intuitive. (See pages 12–21 for an explanation of your Birth Number, and pages 22–23 for an analysis of your secondary Birth Number, if one exists for you.)

The Christian nativity. Your birth number reveals your Life Path and what you were brought into the world to do.

WHAT IT MEANS

Your Birth Number tells you what you have been brought into this world to explore and to find out—it is your Life Path revealed. It is where your soul resides, and is what motivates you. It is the underlying force in everything you do, even if you aren't conscious of it. Your Birth Number also tells you what your innate skills and talents are.

HOW IT CAN HELP YOU

By knowing your Birth Number—your genetic character, if you like—you will have a better understanding of where you are coming from, the underlying motivation that drives you, and your basic instinctive nature. This can be a great help when you need to make important life decisions, especially in the work realm.

For instance, suppose 8 is your Birth Number. This number is all about power, control, willpower, and individuality. Say you are offered a job that requires you to take orders, and be obedient and submissive to your superiors. Knowing now what you do about your inherent nature, do you think you would be happy in this job? According to your Birth Number, the answer is a resounding no. Think of how much grief and stress you just saved yourself by doing this quick calculation.

> ▲ If your Birth Number is 6, chances are that you are a born performer, and are happiest when all eyes are on you.

OTHER PEOPLE'S NUMBERS

Not only can you figure out your own Birth Number and thereby ascertain your own basic nature, you can also get a glimpse into anyone else's basic nature—so long as you know their birth date, that is. By working out your romantic partner's Birth Number, for instance, you can discover his or her basic motivation. This will allow you to have a better understanding of his or her emotions, which will no doubt lead to a stronger and more supportive relationship.

FULL NAME NUMBER

Most people consider a name to be nothing more than a label, but the reality is very different. The name you are born with is your personal talisman. It protects your identity, and connects you with the vibrational powers of the previous generation. Your full name number is the number derived from the name you were given at birth. It can be said to represent the Freudian ego as the exposed and conscious outer self. This number tells you how you present yourself to the outside world—and what others see.

Using the number calculator (see chart opposite), look up the numerical value of each letter of your full name. For instance, if your name were John Robert Smith, the letters would have numerical values as follows:

J O H N   R O B E R T   S M I T H
1 6 8 5   9 6 2 5 9 2   1 4 9 2 8

Add the numbers together:
1 + 6 + 8 + 5 + 9 + 6 + 2 + 5 + 9 + 2 + 1 + 4 + 9 + 2 + 8 = 77

Add the digits of the total together:
7 + 7 = 14

Repeat if necessary to reduce the number to a single digit:
1 + 4 = 5

Thus, your Full Name Number would be 5. Fourteen would be your secondary number, which could be used to flesh out your Full Name Number reading. (See pages 12–21 for an explanation of your Full Name Number, and pages 22–23 for an analysis of your secondary Full Name Number, if one exists for you.)

The name you are given at birth is used to calculate your Full Name Number. It can tell you what sort of person other people think you are.

NUMBER CALCULATOR								
1	2	3	4	5	6	7	8	9
A	B	C	D	E	F	G	H	I
J	K	L	M	N	O	P	Q	R
S	T	U	V	W	X	Y	Z	

The Hindu god Ganesh is revered as a remover of obstacles. A secondary Full Name Number of 14 indicates that you will overcome obstacles in your life.

WHAT IT MEANS

Your Full Name Number reveals your outer personality—how you present yourself to the outside world. It tells you how most people see you, and their likely impressions of you. This number is especially relevant to your career. It does not, however, tell you how the intimates in your life—those who know your real, inner personality—see you; this information is revealed by your Known Name Number (see pages 28–29).

HOW IT CAN HELP YOU

Knowing and understanding how others perceive you can help you in many facets of your life. In the workplace, for example, it can help prepare you for colleagues' reactions to your ideas, thereby making your presentation of these ideas more succinct. In a more general sense, knowing how others think of you can help you live up to their expectations—if you so desire. Or, if you discover that others attribute an unfavorable characteristic to you, you can always make an effort to change your ways—or your name (see pages 30–31).

OTHER PEOPLE'S NUMBERS

It can also be helpful to know and understand the façade that others are presenting to the outside world. For example, if you are going for a job interview, it would certainly be helpful to be able to anticipate the interviewer's personality, which is bound to inform his or her interviewing style. Being familiar with, and having an understanding of, the outer personalities of your friends, acquaintances, and co-workers can also improve your relationship with them.

KNOWN NAME NUMBER

Your known name is the name your lover, your family, and your close friends call you. It can be a nickname, a shortened form of your full name—even just an initial or your last name. The number that is derived from the letters of this name represents what Freud called the id: the hidden or unconscious self, or your inner personality.

First you must identify your known name. Your full name may be John Robert Smith, but everyone may not necessarily know you by that name. You may even be known by a few different names—perhaps your wife calls you John, for example, but your friends call you Bobby. By calculating the numerological values of each of these known names, you can find out which aspects of your personality are most valued. Let us look at an example.

Use the number calculator to find your Known Name Numbers. Add together the numbers of each of your known names, as illustrated below.

J O H N   B O B B Y
1 6 8 5   2 6 2 2 7

To calculate the Known Name Number for John, add the appropriate numbers together:

$$1 + 6 + 8 + 5 = 20$$
$$2 + 0 = 2$$

Thus, 2 is the number for the known name John; this number relates to artistic abilities and inventiveness.

To calculate the Known Name Number for Bobby, add the numbers together:

$$2 + 6 + 2 + 2 + 7 = 19$$
$$1 + 9 = 10$$
$$1 + 0 = 1$$

Thus, 1 is the number for the known name Bobby, relating to strength and activity.

This reading tells us that John's wife, who calls him John, values the artistic side of him, whereas his close friends, who call him Bobby, admire his strength and energy. He probably reveals the softer side of his personality to his wife, and the more adventurous side to his friends. (See pages 12–21 for an explanation of your Known Name Number, and pages 22–23 for an analysis of your secondary Known Name Number, if one exists for you.)

WHAT IT MEANS

Your Known Name Number is essentially your inner personality—the real you. You may show different sides of yourself to different people at different times, but your core personality is who you really are. Chances are, only those with whom you are intimate—your family, close friends, and lover—know you in this way.

HOW IT CAN HELP YOU

Sometimes, we are so busy being so many things to so many people that we forget who we really are, and what truly makes us happy in this life. By ignoring or forgetting about our true selves, we can become profoundly unhappy without ever realizing why. Knowing your Known Name Number and the characteristics associated with it can help you make sure that you never lose sight of the real you, helping you to remain faithful to yourself as well as to your lover, friends, and family.

OTHER PEOPLE'S NUMBERS

Knowing other people's Known Name Numbers and their associated characteristics can be of use in many spheres of our lives, particularly in our relationships. Suppose,

If your Known Name Number is 2, you are likely to reveal your inner artistic side to those who know you best. (Reproduction of a painting by F. H. Kaemmerer.)

for example, that you are currently in a new relationship. It is still at the beginning stages, and so you and your partner are in the process of getting to know each other. Knowing your partner's Known Name Number can give you a fast track into his or her true personality, and can help you ascertain how he or she is really feeling. This type of information can help you become truly intimate more quickly, bringing the two of you closer together in a meaningful, honest way.

CHANGING YOUR NAME

According to Western numerology, a person's name is the code that encrypts his or her essential character. If you change your name, this will result in a change of the vibrations and energies that surround you. As this is the case, such a decision should not be taken lightly. If you do decide to take the plunge, however, the best advice is to choose a name that feels right to you intuitively, and then calculate the numerological meaning of this name to make sure that it has the qualities that you seek. Finally, be sure that you wish to discard the vibrations given off by your old name number—and that you can live up to those given off by the new one.

Many well-known personalities have changed their names at some point in their lives, or have adopted nicknames that reflect their famous personae. Maria Sklodowska, for example, changed her first name to Marie and later became known as Marie Curie after marriage. So her Full Name Number was 1 (bright, tenacious) and her Known Name Number became 3 (energetic, hardworking).

Maria Sklodowska became Marie Curie with a Known Name Number of 3, indicating that she was hardworking—appropriate for a Nobel Prize winner.

FULL NAME NUMBER

As we have already seen, our career is associated with our Full Name Number (see pages 26–27). By changing our full name—the name we were given at birth—we can help ease ourselves into a new career, or change the way we present ourselves to our work colleagues. For example, suppose Jane Brown wishes to make a career change. We know from her Full Name Number of 3 that she is disciplined and successful in her present job. The problem is, she feels more like a 2: artistic and creative. She decides that she may want to change to a more creative job, and would like her Full Name Number to help her channel her creative energies toward this goal. So how can Jane Brown change her Full Name Number of 3 to a 2? One way to do so is to add an initial to her

name: Jane Brown can become Jane H. Brown (with the addition of the "H," which is an 8, the 3 becomes an 11 (3 + 8), which is then reduced to a 2). Thus, Jane Brown has reconfigured her Known Name Number vibrations to ready herself for her new career. Other options for her would have been to add a complete middle name, or change her first or last name.

KNOWN NAME NUMBER

Perhaps you feel like you have outgrown a nickname, or that a name that others affectionately call you simply does not suit your personality. You will feel much better about yourself if you change your known name so that your corresponding Known Name Number reflects your true personality. Let's use Jane Brown again as an example. Suppose people have always called her Janey—a number 1, which is strong and active—but she has always felt more like a 7: spiritual and introverted. If

we remove the "e" from the end of Jane, this would make her name Jan—a 7, which is a much more spiritual and intuitive number. Making this change is bound to make her feel better; she will finally feel that she is being true to her inner self.

Your Known Name Number also relates to your relationships (see pages 28–29). Suppose your Known Name Number is 7, which tells you that you are restless but thoughtful in your relationships, but the truth is that you are lively and pleasure-seeking in that regard—more like a 5. By changing your known name, and thus your Known Name Number, you can ensure that you are surrounded by the correct numerical vibrations.

VOWELS AND CONSONANTS

The vowels and consonants in both our full and known names have specific meanings that govern certain areas of our lives. For example, the first vowel in a person's full name can tell us what motivates him or her in his or her career, while the first vowel in a person's known name tells us what he or she is hiding in his or her relationships.

The chart opposite gives an at-a-glance reference for the numbers associated with each of the vowels, as well as a brief reading of their meanings in the contexts of relationships and careers.

▼ A 19th-century sampler with alphabet and numbers. The vowels and consonants in our names can uncover our secrets and real motivations.

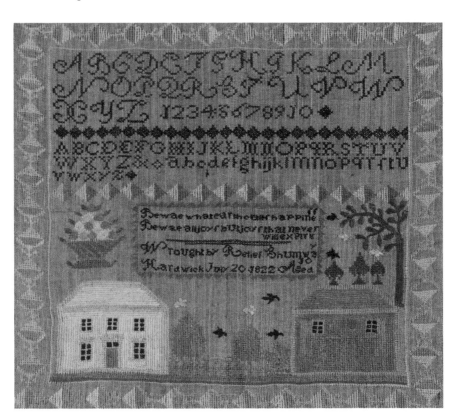

THE MEANING OF THE VOWELS

Vowel	Number	Relationship	Career
A	1	A need to control	Innovation and creativity
E	5	Indulgence and pleasure	Entrepreneurial skills
I	9	A love of danger, reckless behaviour	Communication and expression
O	6	A need for reassurance and a reluctance to trust	Trust and determination
U	3	A need for independence	Energy and talent

Take our old example of John Robert Smith, known to his friends as Bobby. Both his Full Name and Known Name Numbers have "O" as the first vowel. The letter "O" corresponds to the number 6, which is the number of romance, love, and devotion. From his full name (which relates to his career), we know that his motivation at work derives from determination and trust. From his known name (which relates to his relationships), we can guess that Bobby is hiding a fear of falling in love. He is reluctant to commit himself to a romantic relationship, and needs his space and freedom.

LONG-TERM GOALS

If you add up the total of the vowels in your full name, you will arrive at your long-term goals. For example, John Robert Smith's vowel total is:

O + O + E + I
$6 + 6 + 5 + 9 = 26$
$2 + 6 = 8$

Thus, the number 8 is representative of John's long-term career path; 8 is the number of willpower, individuality, and intensity. This reading tells us that John's path will be difficult, but obtainable, so long as he maintains his vision and does not compromise. He will do well in any field of the law or the military—he could even combine the two and become a lawyer who specializes in military law.

RELATIONSHIP EXPECTATIONS

Consonants are the open side of our character and, as such, are much easier to interpret than vowels. By adding together the total of the consonants in our known name, we can find out what we expect from our relationships. By adding together the total of the consonants of our full name, we can discover what we expect in our working life. (See pages 38–39 for more about the relationships and careers for each number.)

COLOR AND NUMEROLOGY

Color is much more than a particular shade or hue. Like numbers, each color has its own vibration. Scientific studies have shown that some colors actually have an effect on our nervous system; for example, the color red stimulates us, while the color blue slows us down. It is no wonder that the advertising and entertainment industries employ colors to create certain moods and elicit desired reactions from viewers!

Just as your personal numbers can give you insight into your true self, so certain colors can help you attract positive vibrations into your surroundings. By choosing a color that has a numerical vibration that is compatible with your personal numbers, you can intensify the positive energy you have begun to build around yourself using these numbers.

FROM HEAD TO TOE

Choose the colors you wear to ensure that you send off the right vibrations in certain situations. For instance, if you are enjoying a day on your own, you might wish to wear the color associated with your Birth Number—you will likely feel the most relaxed in the color that reflects your inherent characteristics. If you have a business meeting, however, you are probably best off wearing the color associated with your Full Name Number— so long as that is the image that you wish to project to the people with whom you are meeting. For an outing with your family, close friends, or lover, you will probably be most comfortable wearing the colors that are linked to your Known Name Number.

Once you become more familiar with the system of numerology, you can play around with colors to suit your mood. Perhaps the idea of wearing orange to a business meeting is not suitable—well, you

The Fashionable Lover, 1774. Choose colors and clothing styles that send out the right vibrations to help you achieve what you want in life.

COLORS AND CLOTHING STYLES

1	RED	Sophisticated, unique, daring, fashionable
2	ORANGE	Smart, chic, matching, co-ordinated
3	YELLOW	Relaxed, casual, light
4	GREEN	Practical, neat, orderly
5	BLUE	Sensual, unusual, sexy
6	INDIGO	Modern, patterned, soft
7	VIOLET	Sharp, crisp, natural
8	CRIMSON/PURPLE	Smart, businesslike, expensive
9	WHITE/PINK	Flamboyant, unconventional, youthful

don't have to dress in orange from head to toe. A tie or scarf—or even orange socks—might be enough to tip the balance. If you think a color doesn't suit you, wearing a different shade of it will work just as well.

COLOR AT HOME

By decorating your home using colors that correspond to your personal numbers, you can attract positive vibrations into your most intimate surroundings. The colors in your bedroom should be those associated with your Birth Number, as you will likely find these colors restful on a basic, instinctive level. For those rooms in which you relax and unwind, such as a sitting room or a living room, it is best to use the colors affiliated with your Known Name Number. The rooms in your home that guests are most likely to enter, such as a front foyer or a dining room, are best decorated using colors to reflect your Full Name Number. If the numerologically

correct color for a particular room is not to your liking—a violet kitchen may be a bit much, for example—it will suffice to add details of the required color to the room. A decorative object here, a pillow there, will be enough to ensure the presence of the positive vibrations that you seek.

STYLE AND COLOR

Just as colors are linked to the nine primary numbers, so are clothing styles. By dressing in the style that corresponds to the appropriate personal number for a specific situation, you can amplify the positive vibrations surrounding you and increase your personal power. Dressing in the style that corresponds to your Full Name Number, for example, will ensure that you project the image that you wish to present to others, while wearing clothing of the style that is linked to your Birth Number or your Known Name Number will make you feel comfortable and confident.

LUCKY DATES

In numerology, each day of the week is associated with one or two of the primary numbers, and carries with it an energy that vibrates to that number. Similarly, each year of your life is linked to one of the primary numbers and its accompanying energy. By learning how to read this energy—that is, by figuring out your personal numbers—you can direct your affairs in such a way as to achieve the best possible results.

LUCKY DAYS

SUNDAY	1 & 8	A day of achievement and success
MONDAY	2 & 9	Can be a day of conflict, but also calmness
TUESDAY	3	A day of general activity
WEDNESDAY	4	A day for hard work
THURSDAY	5	A day for physical activity
FRIDAY	6	A day for thought
SATURDAY	7	A day for learning

Above are the days of the week, their associated numbers, and a description of what one might expect each day to be like. Using this information, we can increase our good fortune by planning certain events on the most auspicious days for them. As well, because we know what to expect on each day, we can prepare ourselves for any potential difficulties that we might encounter. For example, suppose someone named Paul Smith wishes to plan a business meeting. His Full Name Number (the number linked to his career) is 2, so Monday is probably the best day for the meeting to take place. But because Monday can be a day for arguments and conflict, he should make a special effort to ensure that he and the other attendees work together calmly and co-operatively.

From your Birth Number, you can calculate which years will be particularly important for you. Suppose you were born on May 28, 1975. This gives you a Birth Number of 1. From the chart below, we can see that your 10th, 19th, 28th, 37th, and 46th years will be particularly joyous or noteworthy.

LUCKY YEARS

1	10th, 19th, 28th, 37th, 46th
2	11th, 20th, 29th, 38th, 47th
3	12th, 21st, 30th, 39th, 48th
4	13th, 22nd, 31st, 40th, 49th
5	14th, 23rd, 32nd, 41st, 50th
6	15th, 24th, 33rd, 42nd, 51st
7	16th, 25th, 34th, 43rd, 52nd
8	17th, 26th, 35th, 44th, 53rd
9	18th, 27th, 36th, 45th, 54th

◄ A 15th-century German woodcut of a magic calendar used for determining which days will be lucky.

COMPATIBLE PARTNERS

By now it should come as no surprise that the relationships in your life—professional and otherwise—will be better if your numbers are compatible. Each of the nine primary numbers is affiliated with specific personal qualities. When looking for true love, a strong friendship, or any type of mutually beneficial relationship, it can help to ascertain whether your Known Name Number is compatible with that of your potential partner or friend.

A potential partner's Known Name Number can help you decide whether to pursue a romance.

Of course, you and your potential partner or friend need not share the same Known Name Number in order to be compatible; indeed, different Known Name Numbers usually make for spicy, interesting relationships! A look at the person's character traits in relationships will, however, let you know what you are getting into, and will help you decide whether or not you wish to proceed (see opposite). Certain numbers are particularly compatible with others in the romantic sphere. The chart below left shows the best possible romantic matches.

If you are thinking about entering into a business partnership, you should always look at the Full Name Number of your prospective partner and make sure that you can work with someone with the associated character traits. The chart below shows compatible business partners. Each of the nine primary numbers is also linked to specific careers (see opposite).

COMPATIBLE IN LOVE								
1	2	3	4	5	6	7	8	9
4	5	6	7	8	9	1	2	3

COMPATIBLE IN BUSINESS								
1	2	3	4	5	6	7	8	9
6	7	8	9	1	2	3	4	5

RELATIONSHIPS AND CAREERS

No.	Relationship traits		Associated careers
1	Imaginative, strong, independent, active		Design, inventing, teaching, writing, project management
2	Kind, gentle, supportive, loving		Nursing, any area of hospitality, art, therapy, accounting, collecting
3	Controlling, energetic, independent, teacher		Entrepreneur, business, sales, communicating, anything to do with the arts
4	Enduring, reliable, trustworthy, unconventional		Science, mathematics, architecture, engineering, anything to do with buildings, electricity, computers, or technology
5	Pleasure-loving, indulgent, fun, easygoing		Public relations, advertising, acting, journalism, management, anything to do with science, research, or entertainment in a managerial position
6	Caring, articulate, steadfast, enduring		Fashion, theater, charity work, beautician, modeling, music, hairdressing, anything to do with caring for others
7	Intuitive, romantic, sympathetic, thoughtful		Healing, therapy, counseling, clairvoyance, astrology, music, anything to do with being self-employed and running own business
8	Intense, passionate, enthusiastic, impetuous		The military, law, business, financial sector, politics, engineering, banking
9	Dynamic, sophisticated, flamboyant, liberal		Music, hypnotism, exploration, travel, clairvoyance, healing, writing

NUMEROLOGY AND ASTROLOGY

Astrology and numerology are similar systems in that they are both used as tools to uncover the mysteries of life. Both systems are highly intricate, and both are based on mathematical truths that reveal the deeper universal order from which the fabric of life is woven. The primary belief that lies at the heart of astrology is that everything—from all living beings to the planets and stars—is interconnected within a spiritual, energetic relationship.

The planets symbolize the universal characteristics that human beings possess. Mars, for example, symbolizes the warrior. The signs in astrology are named after corresponding star constellations, and act as descriptions of how the planetary characters express their energies. For instance, the astrological sign of Aries, which is linked to the planet Mars, is associated with independence and risk-taking. So if you know your astrological

> A 16th-century Arabic manuscript showing the interrelationship of the Earth, the heavenly saints, the zodiac, and the phases of the Moon.

sign, you can look up its associated number to gain a greater understanding of your nature. Below is a list of the nine primary numbers, together with their corresponding signs and planets.

PLANETS AND ASTROLOGICAL SIGNS

No.	Planet and symbol		Astrological sign and symbol	
1	☉	THE SUN	♌	LEO
2	☽	THE MOON	♋	CANCER
3	♃	JUPITER	♐	SAGITTARIUS
4	♅	URANUS	♒	AQUARIUS
5	☿	MERCURY	♊ ♍	GEMINI / VIRGO
6	♀	VENUS	♉ ♎	TAURUS / LIBRA
7	♆	NEPTUNE	♓	PISCES
8	♄	SATURN	♑	CAPRICORN
9	♂	MARS	♈ ♏	ARIES / SCORPIO

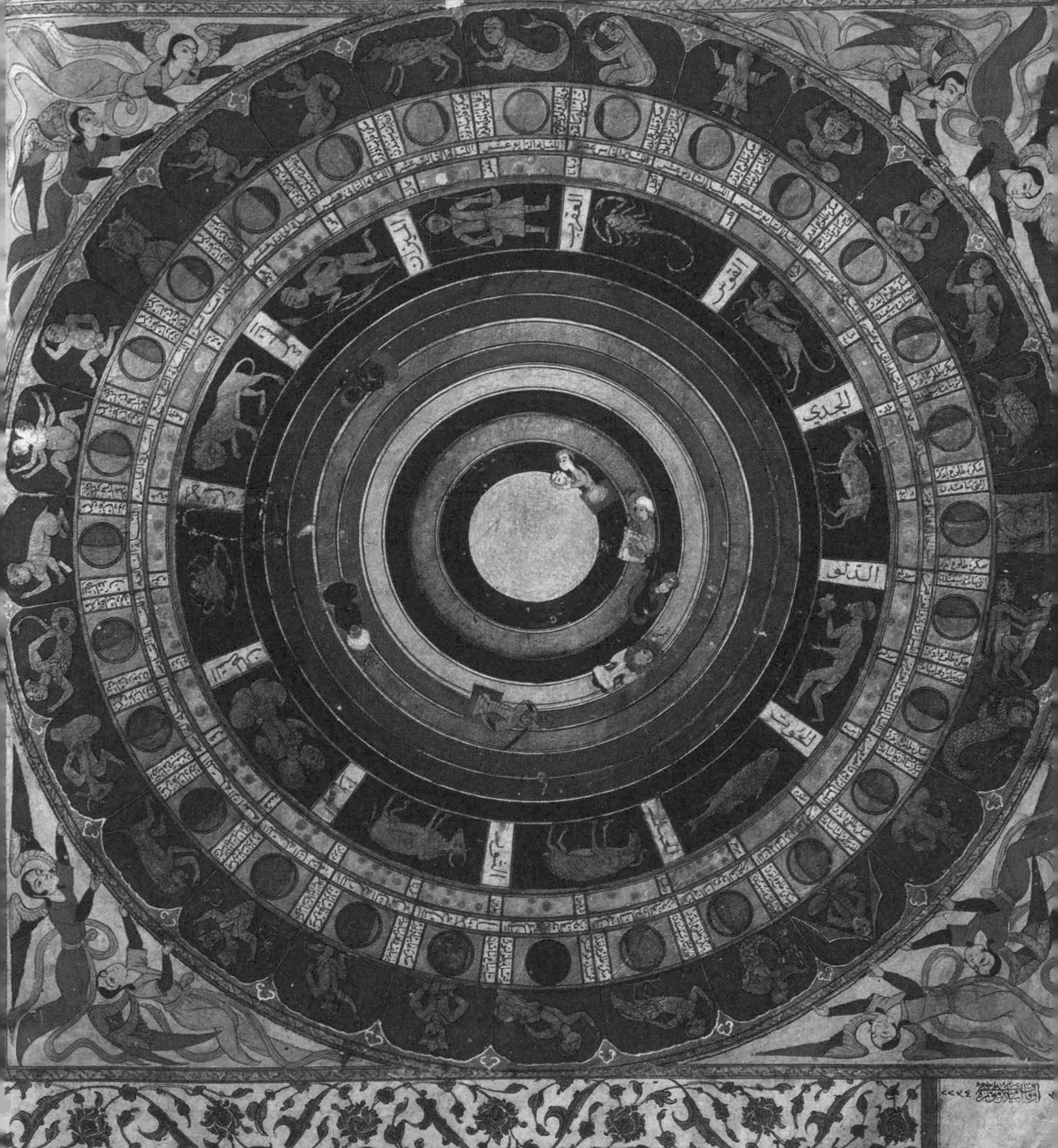

TABLETS OF FATE

Ancient numerology was less concerned with character analysis than with divination. One of the more popular means of divination of the times was the Tablets of Fate, numbered shapes that were used to foretell the outcome of future events and to give divinatory advice.

Each tablet has its own area of concern: the Earth tablet is used for assessing whether you should ask the question at all; the Moon tablet is used for questions about the environment; the tablet of Venus is consulted regarding questions relating to romance; the Sun tablet is used for questions about time and the future; the tablet of Mars should be asked career-related questions; the tablet of Jupiter is meant for questions relating to luck and fortune; and the tablet of Mercury can be asked travel and communications questions.

USING THE TABLETS

In ancient times, the tablets would be printed on a thin sliver of bone or leather. If you are making your own tablets, however, a 5-inch (13cm) square of card cut into the appropriate shape with the numbers written upon it will do. Stick a toothpick or a pencil through the middle of it so that you can spin it.

Use each tablet as follows: ask your question, then spin the card, close your eyes, and stop the card from spinning by placing your finger firmly upon it. The answer to your question is based on the number your finger has landed upon and how the number appears to you: upright or reversed. If the position of the number is unclear—if it lands on its side, for example—you should try again until you get a clear direction. Before you ask any questions, however, you must always refer first to the Tablet of Earth. This is the basic tablet that tells you whether it is a good time to ask your question—and whether you should be asking it at all.

▲ Colored engraving of an armillary sphere, a model of the rings of the celestial sphere.

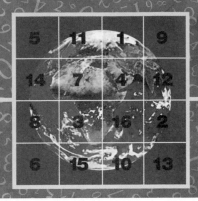

THE TABLET OF THE EARTH

No.	Upright	Reversed
1	Yes, now	Wait 1 day
2	Try tomorrow	Wait 2 days
3	Think very carefully before you ask	Wait 3 days
4	You already know the answer	Wait 4 days
5	Simplify your question	Wait 5 days
6	Act quickly	Wait 6 days
7	Wait a little while before asking	Wait 7 days
8	Change your question	Wait 8 days
9	You aren't in the right frame of mind to ask	Wait 9 days
10	The answer will clarify things	Wait 10 days
11	The answer will only cause you upset	Wait 11 days
12	The answer will surprise you	Wait 12 days
13	The answer will delight you	Wait 13 days
14	Ask only one question today	Wait 2 weeks
15	Question why you want to know	Wait a month
16	If you do not ask you cannot know	Do not ask ever

QUESTIONS TO ASK

You may ask this tablet questions regarding your environment and immediate surroundings. For example, you can ask such questions as "Should I change my residence?" or "Can I redecorate without losing the warm atmosphere I have created?"

THE TABLET OF THE MOON

No.	Upright	Reversed
1	Leave things as they are	Listen to your inner voice
2	You need to change yourself first	Change nothing
3	Your advice is faulty	Are you clear about your objectives?
4	You need your partner's help	Go it alone
5	You already know the answer	Ask again tomorrow
6	Act quickly	Wait 6 days and ask again
7	Be more trusting	Trust no one at this time
8	Change your question	It is not possible at this time
9	Rephrase your question and ask again	Be more patient
10	Look for an unlikely solution	Be wary of easy solutions
11	Pay attention to the details	You have missed something important
12	Yes, if you are thoughtful	Do not undertake any changes
13	Yes, go ahead	Be very cautious
14	Go wild	Be more practical
15	Be active and reckless	Be careful and proceed slowly
16	If you do not ask you cannot know	Tell no one

▶ QUESTIONS TO ASK

As might be expected, the Tablet of Venus should be asked questions pertaining to romantic relationships. This includes questions about a present romantic relationship, as well as those regarding a relationship you hope to have in the future.

THE TABLET OF VENUS

No.	Upright	Reversed
1	Lasting love	Dying love
2	Disagreements	Agreements
3	You won't fool your beloved	You may well fool your beloved
4	Try flattery	Do not try flattery
5	Be hasty	Do not be reckless
6	Blame yourself	Blame your beloved
7	You are wrong to be jealous	You are right to be jealous
8	Work hard to attain your heart's desire	There is nothing you can do at this time
9	Be more serious about this	Lighten up a little
10	Your beloved is thinking of you	Your beloved is not thinking of you
11	This will pass	This is permanent
12	Your beloved misunderstood you	Your beloved knows you too well
13	Your beloved can be trusted	Your beloved cannot be trusted
14	Why are you doubtful?	You are right to be doubtful
15	Speak your mind	Keep silent at this time
16	You have found your soul mate	You are in danger of losing your soul mate

TABLETS OF FATE

THE TABLET OF THE SUN

No.	Upright	Reversed
1	In a while	In 1 year
2	Never	Most likely never
3	Very unlikely	It is possible if you don't interfere
4	Soon	Not so soon
5	Immediately	A very long time away
6	Be patient	You are right to wait
7	Next month	Not for a few months
8	Things will gradually change	Things will suddenly change
9	It will improve quickly	It will worsen quickly
10	In two weeks	Not for at least a month
11	Sooner than you want	Later than you want
12	Next week	Tomorrow, but are you ready?
13	In three days	In three months
14	Don't ask at this time	What will you do when you know?
15	Ask again tomorrow	Do not ask again ever
16	Yes, very soon	Not for a long time

THE TABLET OF MARS

No.	Upright	Reversed
1	Changes are imminent	There will be no change
2	Be patient and you will be rewarded	You will not get any recognition
3	Don't cheat	Be very cautious
4	Your star is ascending	Your star is descending
5	Be more trusting	Trust no one at this time
6	You must put in more effort	You must put in more time
7	Your ideas will be accepted	Your ideas will be rejected
8	Work as part of a team	Work alone for the time being
9	You do not have all the facts	You have overlooked something
10	You are being groomed	You are being ignored
11	It is for the best	It is for the worst
12	You will attain great wealth	You are stagnating

▶ In Chinese astrology, each year is governed by a particular animal with its own characteristics. As with the Tablet of Mars, Chinese horoscopes can be used to divine the most auspicious time to make career decisions.

THE TABLET OF JUPITER

No.	Upright	Reversed
1	You are very lucky	You will experience misfortune
2	A surprise awaits you	You have to put something back
3	You will be rewarded	You can only work hard
4	You will be remembered	You will be forgotten
5	A new friend is waiting	An old friend is waiting
6	This is a good day for you	Delay everything until tomorrow
7	Be more open	Be less trusting
8	It will all turn out right	You will be disappointed

◀ Like the Tablet of Jupiter, the Wheel of Fortune tarot card can be used to answer questions about your destiny involving gain and loss.

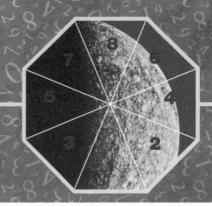

THE TABLET OF MERCURY

No.	Upright	Reversed
1	You will have a good journey	You will have a bad journey
2	Good news awaits	Bad news awaits
3	Don't delay	Put everything off
4	You already know the answer	Be very wary
5	Don't question, just go	You must be honest with yourself
6	Tomorrow you will know	You are not ready yet
7	You received good advice	You received bad advice
8	You will be happy when you get there	Don't go

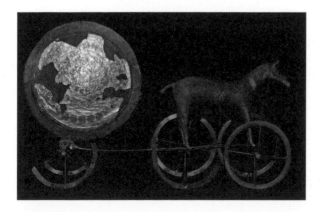

◄ The Trundholm sun chariot, c. 1450 BC. In Norse mythology, the Sun rested on a chariot pulled through the heavens by a horse, represented by the rune "Raido." Like the Tablet of Mercury, Raido signifies travel.

TABLETS OF FATE

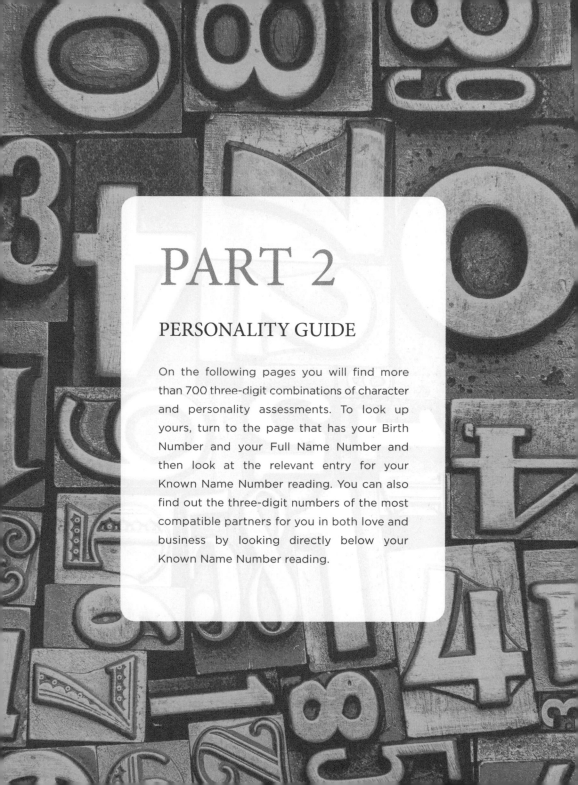

PART 2

PERSONALITY GUIDE

On the following pages you will find more than 700 three-digit combinations of character and personality assessments. To look up yours, turn to the page that has your Birth Number and your Full Name Number and then look at the relevant entry for your Known Name Number reading. You can also find out the three-digit numbers of the most compatible partners for you in both love and business by looking directly below your Known Name Number reading.

Hercules and the Nemean Lion. People with a Birth Number of 1 usually possess great strength and endurance, and make solid leaders because of these qualities.

YOUR UNIQUE PERSONALITY READING

With a Birth Number of 1, you already know that you are extremely confident, as well as bright, honest, and sociable. With a Full Name Number of 1 as well, it is obvious to others that you possess these impressive characteristics. Your Known Name Number reading below is a deeper examination of your personality, and reveals the real you.

KNOWN NAME NUMBER

1 You are the epitome of strength and ambition. Your leadership qualities are renowned and you are busy and creative. Learn to chill out a bit more. You may be too forceful.
LOVE PARTNER 444; BUSINESS PARTNER 666

2 You are strong, busy, and artistic. You work hard and manage to get your ideas across with flair and gusto. You work well if left alone with your creative imagination.
LOVE PARTNER 445; BUSINESS PARTNER 667

3 You are active, creative, and extremely disciplined, which means you will work hard enough to get the job done—no matter what. You are independent and like to be in charge.
LOVE PARTNER 446; BUSINESS PARTNER 668

4 Your innovative but unconventional ideas are ahead of their time—wait for the rest of the world to catch up. One day, you will be proven right. You are practical and logical.
LOVE PARTNER 447; BUSINESS PARTNER 669

5 If you spent as much time and effort on work and close personal relationships as you do on parties and pleasure-seeking, you would accomplish a lot more—and be much happier.
LOVE PARTNER 448; BUSINESS PARTNER 661

6 As a public speaker you have no equal. You know how to put your ideas across and can be very persuasive. You enjoy helping people less fortunate than yourself.
LOVE PARTNER 449; BUSINESS PARTNER 662

7 If the world was looking for another religious prophet, it would come straight to you. You know what makes people tick.
LOVE PARTNER 441; BUSINESS PARTNER 663

8 It's no good butting your head up against a brick wall. You are clever enough to know that, so stop. You have good ideas and people would listen to them if you weren't so difficult.
LOVE PARTNER 442; BUSINESS PARTNER 664

9 Indiana Jones probably had the same three-digit combination as you: active, adventurous, reckless, and courageous. Go for it—the world exists to be conquered by you.
LOVE PARTNER 443; BUSINESS PARTNER 665

▲ Like Galileo, you are full of potentially shocking ideas, Known Name Number 9.

YOUR UNIQUE PERSONALITY READING

A Birth Number of 1 indicates that you were born with confidence to spare. You are a natural leader and a talented innovator. With a Full Name Number of 2, you can be sure that you are seen by others as the creative type. They also see in you a charming and sensitive soul. Only you know if your outer self meshes with your inner self, however. Check your Known Name Number below to see if this is the case.

KNOWN NAME NUMBER

1 You are strong but gentle, energetic but not ruthless, forceful but compassionate. You are the gentle giant, always ready to help others and to be of service. Thank you.
LOVE PARTNER 454; BUSINESS PARTNER 676

2 You move through this world with such confidence and ease that the rest of us are a little jealous. Try to hide a few of your talents so we don't feel so inadequate.
LOVE PARTNER 455; BUSINESS PARTNER 677

3 Everything you do seems so easy because you never panic or get stressed. You are laid-back and extremely confident. All that you have ever wanted has been provided.
LOVE PARTNER 456; BUSINESS PARTNER 678

4 You are an ideas rebel—always looking for the next invention, the next wacky concept or brilliant innovation. You have an enormously imaginative and creative mind. Don't waste it.
LOVE PARTNER 457; BUSINESS PARTNER 679

5 You look like a shady character who hangs around hotel lobbies—until asked to leave, whereupon you reveal that you are really a private investigator. Your disguise is awesome.
LOVE PARTNER 458; BUSINESS PARTNER 671

6 You cannot take on all of the world's ills and not suffer yourself. You care so much that you need to take a break. Learn to be more selective about your causes.
LOVE PARTNER 459; BUSINESS PARTNER 672

7 You are charming, ambitious, and thoughtful. You are also a restless soul. You will travel the world seeking the ultimate answer.
LOVE PARTNER 451; BUSINESS PARTNER 673

8 You are a creative and artistic individual who speaks the truth no matter what the consequences. You may find a little tact helpful. It goes further than bluntness—at times, anyway.
LOVE PARTNER 452; BUSINESS PARTNER 674

9 Galileo was right, but he had to recant. Was he a coward or a hypocrite? You must also choose. You may well be right, but you are well aware that your ideas are shocking to some.
LOVE PARTNER 453; BUSINESS PARTNER 675

BIRTH NUMBER

1

3

FULL NAME NUMBER

YOUR UNIQUE PERSONALITY READING

You love a good challenge, Birth Number 1. Your confident nature may intimidate some people, however, so make sure that you are not being too bossy. Luckily, given your Full Name Number of 3, people see you as an independent person who works hard, and they admire your ability to overcome the odds. Do you really feel this confident and capable, or is it all an act? Check your Known Name Number below to learn more about yourself.

KNOWN NAME NUMBER

1 It might be a good idea occasionally to take some time out to think before you act. You are very headstrong and reckless, and you need to look ahead to the future more often.
LOVE PARTNER 464; BUSINESS PARTNER 686

2 Children adore your ability to motivate them. You have a unique gift and should use it more often. You are an inspirational teacher, and have a gentle charm and strong presence.
LOVE PARTNER 465; BUSINESS PARTNER 687

3 The chances of you actually reading this are remote, as you pretty well know everything already, don't you? But do you really? Isn't there a chance that you may have missed something?
LOVE PARTNER 466; BUSINESS PARTNER 688

4 You are strong, practical, and have tremendous stamina. Stop and think about what you are doing from time to time, although you are a person of action above all else.
LOVE PARTNER 467; BUSINESS PARTNER 689

5 Watch that temper of yours and give people a chance to speak their minds to you in safety. You can be intimidating to others because you are so forthright. Go in peace.
LOVE PARTNER 468; BUSINESS PARTNER 681

6 People trust you, as you have a very gentle way about you. Make sure you don't destroy that trust by being too headstrong or too reckless. You care about others and can be kind.
LOVE PARTNER 469; BUSINESS PARTNER 682

7 You have a talent for knowing exactly what people are thinking. To what use will you put this secret knowledge? Are you to be trusted with the inner thoughts and feelings of others?
LOVE PARTNER 461; BUSINESS PARTNER 683

8 You have carved a niche for yourself through your formidable strength and stamina. Now what are you going to do? Take some time out to answer this question—don't jump the gun.
LOVE PARTNER 462; BUSINESS PARTNER 684

9 We know you like your independence, so what's the trouble? We have no wish to curb your freedom, so stop being so argumentative.
LOVE PARTNER 463; BUSINESS PARTNER 685

BIRTH NUMBER 1

FULL NAME NUMBER 4

YOUR UNIQUE PERSONALITY READING

Those of you with a Birth Number of 1 inherently possess endless energy, stamina, and enthusiasm. Instead of finding you exhausting, however, we know from your Full Name Number of 4 that others see this zest for life as an indication of your robustness and strength. But this isn't the complete picture of your personality—your Known Name Number reading below provides the final piece to the puzzle.

KNOWN NAME NUMBER

1 You cannot fail to succeed, as you have more ideas in a day than we have in a lifetime. You will surely roll some of them into a successful business and be very wealthy one day.
LOVE PARTNER 474; BUSINESS PARTNER 696

2 By being as eccentric as you are, you only draw attention to your unconventional ideas. Better to blend in more if you want to make headway. Learn to adopt a disguise.
LOVE PARTNER 475; BUSINESS PARTNER 697

3 You are very ambitious, but your success will depend upon whether you can learn to be a little more diplomatic and flexible. Can you change? If not, you may become isolated.
LOVE PARTNER 476; BUSINESS PARTNER 698

4 Don't worry—all that effort and hard work will not be in vain. Your reward is coming and your exertions will be praised. Just keep your head down and don't ask—yet.
LOVE PARTNER 477; BUSINESS PARTNER 699

5 Wait a little while and the world will be ready to accept your ideas. Don't push. Don't argue. Be patient. Carry on exactly as you are. It's just a question of time.
LOVE PARTNER 478; BUSINESS PARTNER 691

6 You are strong, steady, and resolute. You work hard, play hard, and get on with the job. You have a reputation for being a bit serious.
LOVE PARTNER 479; BUSINESS PARTNER 692

7 You have quite a knack for being intuitive about all the wrong things. Better to direct your talents to a more appropriate cause and stop interfering where you may not be wanted.
LOVE PARTNER 471; BUSINESS PARTNER 693

8 Ah, the rebel of the numerology world. What can we say to you that you will listen to? Nothing. Carry on the way you are going and you will alienate all your friends.
LOVE PARTNER 472; BUSINESS PARTNER 694

9 White-water rapids hold no fear for you. You have more courage than is needed in this world, and are happiest when bungee jumping, climbing a mountain, or canoeing the Amazon.
LOVE PARTNER 473; BUSINESS PARTNER 695

BIRTH NUMBER

1

5

FULL NAME NUMBER

▲ You can't rescue every stray dog—or person—Known Name Number 6.

YOUR UNIQUE PERSONALITY READING

In its positive aspects, the Birth Number 1 is honest and upright. In its negative aspects, however, it is domineering and bossy, and can be quite intimidating. Those of you with Full Name Numbers of 5 have thankfully learned to keep these negative aspects in check; others see you as socially graceful. Indeed, you are a bit of an enigma. Your Known Name Number below can help you solve your own mystery.

KNOWN NAME NUMBER

1 You are the perfect party organizer. You have a flair for knowing what people need to relax. You can use this talent to run a successful business, or squander it on indulgence.
LOVE PARTNER 484; BUSINESS PARTNER 616

2 You think you are always right, but haven't you overlooked something? Don't you often miss the vital clue because you are in such a rush to get things done? Listen and look more closely.
LOVE PARTNER 485; BUSINESS PARTNER 617

3 You are inquisitive, busy, businesslike, quick, and a born opportunist. No opportunity passes you by without you making a profit from it. You care for your family extremely well.
LOVE PARTNER 486; BUSINESS PARTNER 618

4 Rebellious, impulsive, active, and strong: these are your key words. Take these words not only as praise, but also as a caution. It's time you developed a little bit of tact and diplomacy.
LOVE PARTNER 487; BUSINESS PARTNER 619

5 For some of us, life is a learning experience. For you, however, it is purely fun. This is a life off for you and you can coast as much as you want without concern. Enjoy.
LOVE PARTNER 488; BUSINESS PARTNER 611

6 Taking home stray dogs may seem like a good idea, but your house will quickly fill up with hungry canines. Be more selective, and only rescue those who will appreciate it.
LOVE PARTNER 489; BUSINESS PARTNER 612

7 On the outside, you are busy and sociable; but inside, you are shy and retiring. You handle this obvious imbalance extremely well and are coping adequately.
LOVE PARTNER 481; BUSINESS PARTNER 613

8 Don't be so defensive when criticized. People are trying to help you, not hinder you. Heed what they have to say and you will improve yourself. Don't listen and you will alienate them.
LOVE PARTNER 482; BUSINESS PARTNER 614

9 You like being busy and active, but is it just a distraction to stop you from thinking? You will have to face your inner demons one day.
LOVE PARTNER 483; BUSINESS PARTNER 615

BIRTH NUMBER

1

6

FULL NAME NUMBER

▲ You are a tower of strength and as solid as a rock, Known Name Number 6.

YOUR UNIQUE PERSONALITY READING

With a Birth Number of 1, nothing pleases you more than going out into the world and exercising your formidable creativity. You are a true individual, as well as a leader and innovator. Perhaps others follow you so willingly because they find you trustworthy, as indicated by your Full Name Number of 6. Check your Known Name Number below to complete the picture of the complicated being that you are.

KNOWN NAME NUMBER

1 If you are not a politician, then what are you wasting your time on? You have a caring side that needs an outlet, and politics takes all of your communication skills into account.
LOVE PARTNER 494; BUSINESS PARTNER 626

2 Strong, reliable, and charming—that's you. You'd make a great daytime TV talk show host. You make people feel at ease, and they open up to you in an extraordinary way.
LOVE PARTNER 495; BUSINESS PARTNER 627

3 You can make a fortune simply by being clever at getting your ideas across. You have tremendous communication skills and a wealth of good ideas. Be confident and go for it.
LOVE PARTNER 496; BUSINESS PARTNER 628

4 Many new ideas are ridiculed before they become accepted. This is the nature of things and you cannot fight it. Be patient. Hold fast to your bright vision and you will be rewarded.
LOVE PARTNER 497; BUSINESS PARTNER 629

5 You'd be successful if only you would see projects through. You run out of enthusiasm too quickly. This will improve as you age, but practice some diligence in the meantime.
LOVE PARTNER 498; BUSINESS PARTNER 621

6 People rely heavily on your strength and steadfastness. But who finds time for you? Start thinking about yourself for once—you need a confidante and companion too.
LOVE PARTNER 499; BUSINESS PARTNER 622

7 You should be writing books like this one. You have the talent, the intuition, and the skill. So what's holding you back? Ah, so you lack confidence. Get some and go for it.
LOVE PARTNER 491; BUSINESS PARTNER 623

8 You are ambitious, successful, resolute, and creative. You are also a bit intense and have trouble getting along with people. Treat us a little more kindly please.
LOVE PARTNER 492; BUSINESS PARTNER 624

9 You are more than happy to descend into the very jaws of hell to rescue others. Take care lest your love of danger gets you into trouble.
LOVE PARTNER 493; BUSINESS PARTNER 625

YOUR UNIQUE PERSONALITY READING

You do not take orders well, Birth Number 1. You always want to be in charge, as you know you are usually the best person for the job. If 7 is your Full Name Number, these innate characteristics are confirmed; others constantly come to you for advice because they believe in you, and see you as mentally superior. Your Known Name Number below can tell you a bit more about your true colors.

KNOWN NAME NUMBER

1 You are determined and headstrong, and have a great sense of purpose. You have valuable work to do and need to get on with it. There will come a time when you need to teach.
LOVE PARTNER 414; BUSINESS PARTNER 636

2 Channel your energies into travel. Seek to learn about the world we live in and how you may be of help. You are capable of charming the whole world if you learn to smile more often.
LOVE PARTNER 415; BUSINESS PARTNER 637

3 You must not expect everyone to do your bidding all the time. Allow others to express themselves more, and you will be surprised at how much they are drawn to you.
LOVE PARTNER 416; BUSINESS PARTNER 638

4 If you must rebel, at least find something worthwhile to fight against. You are intuitive and strong, and need to concern yourself with the big issues of the day rather than the details.
LOVE PARTNER 417; BUSINESS PARTNER 639

5 If you concern yourself only with pleasure, make sure it is for the benefit of others as well as yourself. You are headstrong, and seek to always have your own way.
LOVE PARTNER 418; BUSINESS PARTNER 631

6 Your inner strengths are directed toward caring for others. You have a natural, intuitive way of communicating advice and help, which comes from a very real and secure base.
LOVE PARTNER 419; BUSINESS PARTNER 632

7 With 7 as both an inner and outer number, you are both blessed and cursed with an almost telepathic knowledge of what others are thinking. Use this power wisely.
LOVE PARTNER 411; BUSINESS PARTNER 633

8 If you learn to curb your stubborn streak, you will find success in this life—but can you do this? You are a very intense individual who may be perceived as difficult and rebellious.
LOVE PARTNER 412; BUSINESS PARTNER 634

9 If anyone needed a hero, it might well be you they would turn to. You are courageous and determined—but you can also be quarrelsome.
LOVE PARTNER 413; BUSINESS PARTNER 635

YOUR UNIQUE PERSONALITY READING

With a Birth Number of 1, you are above average in intelligence, which only adds to your innate confidence. You need to be careful not to intimidate others, and should focus on being more diplomatic. This will be difficult, however, as you enjoy speaking your mind—indeed, others expect this sort of behavior from you, given that your Full Name Number is 8. Your Known Name Number below offers a glimpse into your inner personality.

KNOWN NAME NUMBER

1 You are very ambitious and aggressive. This is fine, just so long as you treat people kindly as your career progresses. If you don't, you will never truly enjoy the fruits of your labor.
LOVE PARTNER 424; BUSINESS PARTNER 646

2 Paranoia isn't a normal state to be in. They aren't out to get you, so relax. Be at one with your universe. It's okay to be you and to allow others to see your vulnerable side. Be trusting.
LOVE PARTNER 425; BUSINESS PARTNER 647

3 You like to control every aspect of life around you, and you seem to be able to get away with this terrible behavior. This is probably because of your creative genius. Lucky you.
LOVE PARTNER 426; BUSINESS PARTNER 648

4 No matter what anyone else says, you always go your own sweet way. Fair enough, just so long as you aren't sulking. Be your own person, but do it all for the right reasons.
LOVE PARTNER 427; BUSINESS PARTNER 649

5 They see you as mysterious and brooding, secretive and enigmatic. Is this the real you, or have you learned to hide your true self? Most of this is an act; try being softer.
LOVE PARTNER 428; BUSINESS PARTNER 641

6 You might be doing it your way and getting somewhere. But how about trying a little tact? You might get there quicker and with less stress. You have a silver tongue.
LOVE PARTNER 429; BUSINESS PARTNER 642

7 You hammer away at life, and just when things seem at their worst a miracle happens and saves you. You are one very lucky individual.
LOVE PARTNER 421; BUSINESS PARTNER 643

8 Just because you are creative and artistic doesn't mean you can behave rudely or unkindly. You may be an intellectual giant, but you should learn to be a loving one as well.
LOVE PARTNER 422; BUSINESS PARTNER 644

9 You are like an old-fashioned movie tycoon with a big cigar and a tyrant's ego. You can be ruthless. Lighten up a bit and give others a chance to speak. You might like what you hear.
LOVE PARTNER 423; BUSINESS PARTNER 645

BIRTH NUMBER **1**

9 FULL NAME NUMBER

▲ You are as frenzied as a tornado, Known Name Number 3.

YOUR UNIQUE PERSONALITY READING

The Birth Number 1 makes for complex and contradictory individuals: it is the sign of the saint and the tyrant, the savior and the dictator. If your Full Name Number is 9, you are most likely on the saint and savior side of the fence. You have a great need to express yourself; others may even see you as a great poet. But your inner personality, as shown below in your Known Name Number reading, represents the real you.

KNOWN NAME NUMBER

1 Your determination knows no bounds. You are going to succeed no matter what. The trouble is, what will you do when you get there? Slow down a bit and enjoy the ride.
LOVE PARTNER 434; BUSINESS PARTNER 656

2 Carry your vision with you and be kind to the little people along the way. You will be amply rewarded once you arrive at the place called success if you have behaved decently.
LOVE PARTNER 435; BUSINESS PARTNER 657

3 Whoa! You are a tornado, a tiger, a whirling dervish. You are a blur in people's sights—they can't get a handle on you. Slow down a bit and let's have a look at you.
LOVE PARTNER 436; BUSINESS PARTNER 658

4 You are the wild artist in the attic, the starving poet in the tower. But why? You have enough talent to earn a good living. So why this act? Come on down and be real with us.
LOVE PARTNER 437; BUSINESS PARTNER 659

5 You can't do everything yourself. At some point, you will have to accept some help, be

it from a partner or a colleague. Stop trying to be everything to everyone.
LOVE PARTNER 438; BUSINESS PARTNER 651

6 You are resolute, reckless, courageous, daring, and utterly fearless. That's all fine and well in the jungle, but in everyday life you are in danger of becoming a dinosaur.
LOVE PARTNER 439; BUSINESS PARTNER 652

7 There is no point in playing spiritual games. You are intuitive and psychic, but it is in the use of such knowledge that true power resides. And power can be taken away if used unwisely.
LOVE PARTNER 431; BUSINESS PARTNER 653

8 You are like a wild alley cat—always ready to spit, bite, scratch, or cuss. Relax. Allow yourself to be stroked occasionally.
LOVE PARTNER 432; BUSINESS PARTNER 654

9 I would like to offer you some advice, but you'd bite my head off. I would suggest that you might win more influence if you learned to be a bit more diplomatic and tactful.
LOVE PARTNER 433; BUSINESS PARTNER 655

◄ **The Quiver of Love,** Valentine illustration. Birth Number 2 people tend to be very emotional, and sometimes overly sensitive. Their moods can sway from ecstatic to forlorn in a moment.

YOUR UNIQUE PERSONALITY READING

If 2 is your Birth Number, you are innately a very gentle person, with a strong feminine side. You can also be highly emotional—sometimes to the point of inaction. Your Full Name Number of 1 indicates that others sometimes see you as a bit of a loner; you really must try harder to get along with people, both in your social life and at work. Your Known Name Number reading below will help you understand yourself a bit better.

KNOWN NAME NUMBER

1 Everything you do is based on your intuitive grasp of human nature. This can make you very clever or very cynical. You have great drive, strength, and ambition.
LOVE PARTNER 544; BUSINESS PARTNER 766

2 If you aren't careful, you are in danger of losing touch with reality. Keep your feet planted firmly on the ground and try not to be so dreamy.
LOVE PARTNER 545; BUSINESS PARTNER 767

3 You are wonderful at translating your ideas into positive action; people respect your ability and give you their time because of this. Make sure you remain realistic.
LOVE PARTNER 546; BUSINESS PARTNER 768

4 You may need to tailor your ideas a little to become slightly more conventional. Doing so will get you farther, and shouldn't be seen as betraying your ideals. Don't be so rebellious.
LOVE PARTNER 547; BUSINESS PARTNER 769

5 If you don't settle down to some real work, you will squander all those dreams. You feel compelled to daydream and procrastinate, but you really must get on with it.
LOVE PARTNER 548; BUSINESS PARTNER 761

6 Take some time out to think about what it is you want. You give so much time to others that there really isn't any left for you. Try saying no sometimes.
LOVE PARTNER 549; BUSINESS PARTNER 762

7 It's no good always relying on luck to get you out of trouble. Start being more proactive about the things that need to get done.
LOVE PARTNER 541; BUSINESS PARTNER 763

8 If you stop being quite so intense, you will find work more enjoyable, and you may even become part of a team. This is what you want, so why do you drive people away?
LOVE PARTNER 542; BUSINESS PARTNER 764

9 You are very determined and can swamp people. Give others a little more space and they will respond to you better. You are very lively and need to calm down a little.
LOVE PARTNER 543; BUSINESS PARTNER 765

BIRTH NUMBER 2

FULL NAME NUMBER 2

▲ Now is the time to go for what you want, Known Name Number 9.

YOUR UNIQUE PERSONALITY READING

With both your Birth Number and your Full Name Number as 2, you really are as you seem: charming, sensitive, and gentle. You get along well with others, and are a great friend. People are always leaning on you for support. But only you know how you really feel about your designated role as nurturer. Perhaps you should spend more time taking care of yourself. Your Known Name Number reading below may shed some light on this.

KNOWN NAME NUMBER

1 You have an amazing ability to think laterally. Use this talent to increase your creativity and you will go far. You are anxious for recognition rather than money.
LOVE PARTNER 554; BUSINESS PARTNER 776

2 People may well take advantage of you if you don't learn to stand up for yourself a bit more. Your quiet, thoughtful nature is misinterpreted as weakness. Be tougher.
LOVE PARTNER 555; BUSINESS PARTNER 777

3 Your charm will get you as far as you want to go, and your artistic talent will provide a good living. But stop trying to be in charge all the time—allow others to speak up more.
LOVE PARTNER 556; BUSINESS PARTNER 778

4 Keep plugging away at your dreams and you will get there. The time just isn't quite right for your unconventional vision. It would be criminal to give up now—you're nearly there.
LOVE PARTNER 557; BUSINESS PARTNER 779

5 Unless you stand to inherit a lot of money, you need to start earning a living or you will become a scrounger. Go out and get a job. You are growing old disgracefully.
LOVE PARTNER 558; BUSINESS PARTNER 771

6 People rely on you and trust your judgment. If you learn to use this talent properly, you will have a long and successful career. You need to learn how to speak up about what you know.
LOVE PARTNER 559; BUSINESS PARTNER 772

7 Whatever it is that you are trying to express can only be communicated once you have put it into words internally. You need to speak your words of wisdom to yourself before others.
LOVE PARTNER 551; BUSINESS PARTNER 773

8 You are a unique individual and possess great charm. You can also be stubborn, but people forgive you and like you a great deal. You have a need to express yourself in an artistic way.
LOVE PARTNER 552; BUSINESS PARTNER 774

9 There is something you've always wanted to do, and now is the time to do it. Take your courage in both hands and aim for the stars.
LOVE PARTNER 553; BUSINESS PARTNER 775

YOUR UNIQUE PERSONALITY READING

The Birth Number 2 makes you innately a peacekeeper. You feel alarmed when people are fighting in front of you, and would do anything if they would only kiss and make up. This need to promote harmony is recognized by others; your Full Name Number 3 tells you that you are known as a troubleshooter, and are sought out as a mediator by quarrelling factions. Your Known Name Number below can help you discover if this is the real you.

KNOWN NAME NUMBER

1 There is nothing that holds you back. You are artistic, strong, ambitious, and energetic. You have an aptitude for hard work, and this will always stand you in good stead.
LOVE PARTNER 564; BUSINESS PARTNER 786

2 You are inventive, talented, and thoughtful. If you apply yourself, you will achieve a great deal. You need to toughen up a bit, but the world could certainly use more people like you.
LOVE PARTNER 565; BUSINESS PARTNER 787

3 You wonder why people aren't more drawn to you, and yet you do nothing to encourage them. Your need for independence makes you seem remote. Try to be more approachable.
LOVE PARTNER 566; BUSINESS PARTNER 788

4 You can achieve your vision by hard work, but if you remain so unconventional you will encounter problems. Perhaps you need to make more of an effort to reach out to others.
LOVE PARTNER 567; BUSINESS PARTNER 789

5 You are one of those lucky people who can make money, attract lovers, and influence people—almost without trying. You have a natural gift for charm and sophistication.
LOVE PARTNER 568; BUSINESS PARTNER 781

6 Is there nothing that you won't do for others? You are so kind, so loving, and so helpful that you may feel slightly put upon at times.
LOVE PARTNER 569; BUSINESS PARTNER 782

7 You love travel and will wander forever if you don't put down some roots. You are drawn to foreign places, and have a need to sense and experience other cultures.
LOVE PARTNER 561; BUSINESS PARTNER 783

8 You are artistic, energetic, and successful. You have a marvelous ability to combine the creative with the practical and, although you can be rebellious, you are an efficient hard worker.
LOVE PARTNER 562; BUSINESS PARTNER 784

9 You are managing your quarrelsome nature extremely well, and haven't lost your temper for ages. Well done. You are caring and you make this world a better place.
LOVE PARTNER 563; BUSINESS PARTNER 785

YOUR UNIQUE PERSONALITY READING

You are by nature a diplomatic, peaceful person, but another side of you has a tendency to avoid making decisions. Indeed, your Birth Number 2 is marked by indecision. Thankfully, this is not how others perceive you. If your Full Name Number is 4, then you are seen as possessing a great loyalty toward ideas, which counteracts any hint of indecisiveness. Your true inner personality is revealed below in your Known Name Number reading.

KNOWN NAME NUMBER

1 Without a life partner, you will flounder. You need to be part of a team of two, so get out there and find your soul mate. You may have duties, but you must think of your happiness.
LOVE PARTNER 574; BUSINESS PARTNER 796

2 Don't be frightened to speak your mind. I know you don't like to hurt people's feelings, but you really do need to make some changes. Be less charming and more ruthless.
LOVE PARTNER 575; BUSINESS PARTNER 797

3 You work long hours and are frequently exhausted. Learn to relax a bit more and have some fun. You are in danger of being labeled a workaholic if you carry on at this rate.
LOVE PARTNER 576; BUSINESS PARTNER 798

4 You have a lot of interesting ideas and are good at putting them into realistic outlets. You are creative and inventive, but you need to curb your wilder excesses.
LOVE PARTNER 577; BUSINESS PARTNER 799

5 You need people around you—and you need to be part of a team—so stop pushing them

away. You need them in order to flourish. Try to be a little less concerned with pleasure.
LOVE PARTNER 578; BUSINESS PARTNER 791

6 You should be a counselor, but not a conventional one. You have a natural gift for helping people. You need to find an outlet for this talent, but go for the wacky or the new.
LOVE PARTNER 579; BUSINESS PARTNER 792

7 You have the wonderful ability to surf the cosmos and bring back spiritual ideas that inspire other people. Find an outlet for this incredible talent, and you are bound for success.
LOVE PARTNER 571; BUSINESS PARTNER 793

8 You are driven and goal-oriented. You work like a machine, and expect the same from others. You need to realize that people need to be nurtured in order to get the best from them.
LOVE PARTNER 572; BUSINESS PARTNER 794

9 You must try to find a more diplomatic way to get your ideas across. You must make allowances for the views of others.
LOVE PARTNER 573; BUSINESS PARTNER 795

BIRTH NUMBER **2**

FULL NAME NUMBER **5**

▲ You are at peace with yourself and the world around you, Birth Number 2.

YOUR UNIQUE PERSONALITY READING

What an optimist you are, you of the Birth Number 2! People have accused you of being too idealistic, but you know that it is possible to make the world a better place—if only people would try harder. We know from your Full Name Number of 5 that people see you as charming and graceful, which helps you attain your charitable goals. But are you really as angelic as you seem? Your Known Name Number below reveals your true personality.

KNOWN NAME NUMBER

1 You have a marvelous ability to integrate all the elements of mind, body, and spirit. You set a good example for the rest of us as to how to be both businesslike and creative.
LOVE PARTNER 584; BUSINESS PARTNER 716

2 If you go off on a tangent and don't stick to the job, you will miss out on the success that is rightfully yours. Apply yourself to the task at hand and don't be so dreamy.
LOVE PARTNER 585; BUSINESS PARTNER 717

3 You suffer from apathy or loss of energy at times, and need to watch your diet carefully. You should get more exercise. You need to say thank you to someone who loves you.
LOVE PARTNER 586; BUSINESS PARTNER 718

4 You are not alone. Help is very near—you just haven't looked in the right place yet. Be more adventurous. You have a rebellious side that needs to see more light.
LOVE PARTNER 587; BUSINESS PARTNER 719

5 A few less parties and a few earlier nights and you might achieve a lot more. You are easily led astray. Look at your friends carefully and get rid of the ones that are a bad influence.
LOVE PARTNER 588; BUSINESS PARTNER 711

6 You are well-known as a natural orator. You can be a bit unreliable, though, and may lose respect because of this.
LOVE PARTNER 589; BUSINESS PARTNER 712

7 You are like the fabled hare—quick-moving, shy, determined, and a bit restless. The hare also has a reputation for being ethereal and not quite of this world—like you.
LOVE PARTNER 581; BUSINESS PARTNER 713

8 There is a side of you that you are right to keep hidden: that darker, more mercurially aggressive part. You know you have a sharp tongue. Work on keeping it under control.
LOVE PARTNER 582; BUSINESS PARTNER 714

9 You are determined to earn a reputation as a scoundrel. Perhaps it's time to curb this desire to be thought of as a troublemaker and to start expressing your artistic side.
LOVE PARTNER 583; BUSINESS PARTNER 715

BIRTH NUMBER

2

FULL NAME NUMBER

6

▲ You look for lucky omens and follow your intuition, Known Name Number 7.

YOUR UNIQUE PERSONALITY READING

With a Birth Number of 2, not only are you caring and gentle, you are also extremely intuitive, and possess great insight into the feelings of others. These qualities make you a great parent, sibling, or child. Add these qualities to the fact that your Full Name Number is 6, the number of domestication, and you are quite happy just staying home and caring for your family. Check below to see if your inner personality meshes with this reading.

KNOWN NAME NUMBER

1 If you could gather up the whole world in the palm of your hand and love us, you would be happy. Well, you can't. You would be better off finding a single cause to support.
LOVE PARTNER 594; BUSINESS PARTNER 726

2 You move through this world in a hazy vision of love and peace, like some Sixties hippie. Well, life ain't like that. You need to be more real and to get grounded.
LOVE PARTNER 595; BUSINESS PARTNER 727

3 Inventive, loving, and talented—that's you. You care about people, and can often see ways to help them that they may have overlooked. Keep up the good work.
LOVE PARTNER 596; BUSINESS PARTNER 728

4 You may wonder why people don't take your advice more often when you are so willing to give it. Perhaps they look at the proof of the eating rather than the pudding you offer.
LOVE PARTNER 597; BUSINESS PARTNER 729

5 You have a quick mind, but you need to apply yourself a little more to your goals.

Stop expending your energies on pleasure and start paying more attention to the serious stuff.
LOVE PARTNER 598; BUSINESS PARTNER 721

6 People trust you and bring their problems to you, and you are very good at giving them advice, encouraging them to stand on their own two feet. Do the same for yourself occasionally.
LOVE PARTNER 599; BUSINESS PARTNER 722

7 You don't move through this world like the rest of us. We deal with concrete facts, but you deal with feelings, hunches, and omens.
LOVE PARTNER 591; BUSINESS PARTNER 723

8 You can be obstinate, especially with partners, which is a shame since you also have a loving side. You just have this terrible need to win all arguments.
LOVE PARTNER 592; BUSINESS PARTNER 724

9 You are determined to save the world, the whales, the kangaroos—even if none of them need saving. You devote a lot of energy to lost causes. Start being a little more realistic.
LOVE PARTNER 593; BUSINESS PARTNER 725

YOUR UNIQUE PERSONALITY READING

Some have accused you, Birth Number 2, of avoiding your responsibilities. Deep down, you know this is true, but you put off making important decisions anyway—you just don't want to deal with the pressure. Your Full Name Number of 7 tells us that some might see you as cold and uncaring, even though you're not—you just want someone else to solve the problem. Your Known Name Number reading below shows how you feel about it all.

KNOWN NAME NUMBER

1 You are inventive, spiritual, and ambitious. I do hope you are not going to try to sell me a new religion or cult. You should be aware of the long-term results of your actions.
LOVE PARTNER 514; BUSINESS PARTNER 736

2 You need to watch less TV and get out more. Join a club or two. Go on a vacation. Switch your computer off occasionally. Get some fresh air and exercise. You know what I'm saying.
LOVE PARTNER 515; BUSINESS PARTNER 737

3 You are active, imaginative, and very lucky. With your charm and talent, you can reach heights the rest of us only dream of. So what's holding you back? Be bold and take the plunge.
LOVE PARTNER 516; BUSINESS PARTNER 738

4 Inside you there is a small child crying out that life isn't fair. Just accept that it was never meant to be. The sooner you do, the quicker you can get on with your life. Be strong and real.
LOVE PARTNER 517; BUSINESS PARTNER 739

5 No one can ever quite get a handle on you. You are elusive, a creature of the shadows and moonlight. You are a nebulous entity full of mystery and illusion—and you like it that way.
LOVE PARTNER 518; BUSINESS PARTNER 731

6 You have a rapport with people who need caring and love. The trouble is, you may be one of those people yourself. So who cares for you? Stand up and demand the love you deserve.
LOVE PARTNER 519; BUSINESS PARTNER 732

7 If you were any less grounded, you'd simply float away. Only your partner keeps you on earth, and you should be grateful for that.
LOVE PARTNER 511; BUSINESS PARTNER 733

8 You are one of those rare people who can be in this world but not of it. You are able to put your talents for caring and sharing to use in a very successful and businesslike way. Well done.
LOVE PARTNER 512; BUSINESS PARTNER 734

9 There is something slightly dangerous about you. I wouldn't tell you my problems for fear you might use the information against me. This may, of course, just be your image.
LOVE PARTNER 513; BUSINESS PARTNER 735

BIRTH NUMBER
2

FULL NAME NUMBER
8

YOUR UNIQUE PERSONALITY READING

You of the Birth Number 2 are in touch with your feminine side. You have a wonderfully nurturing personality, lending your friends and lovers virtually endless support and an ever-ready shoulder to cry on. In fact, you are so good with others that you are, as your Full Name Number 8 tells us, a great leader. Everyone knows that sticking with you is a safe bet. Only your Known Name Number can tell you what's going on deep down inside.

KNOWN NAME NUMBER

1 You are a tornado of energy and activity. But is it all show and no substance? Show us that you can really achieve all that you claim and we will be convinced.
LOVE PARTNER 524; BUSINESS PARTNER 746

2 Whatever you turn your hand to comes out right. You could scribble a phone number on a piece of paper and sell it as a masterpiece. You can also be a bit of a schemer.
LOVE PARTNER 525; BUSINESS PARTNER 747

3 You have achieved a great deal by being difficult and intense. Perhaps now is the time to ease up a bit and relax. You may make some enemies if you don't learn to be more pleasant.
LOVE PARTNER 526; BUSINESS PARTNER 748

4 You are rebellious when there is simply no need to be. You have the strength of character to throw off your old image of being a troublemaker and start doing some hard work.
LOVE PARTNER 527; BUSINESS PARTNER 749

5 You are acquiring a reputation for being unreliable because you take so much time off. This affects both work and relationships. Figure out why you need to escape so often.
LOVE PARTNER 528; BUSINESS PARTNER 741

6 Your artistic side is being displayed in a very individualistic way. Whether this is working for you only you can judge. If it is, keep on being wacky. If it isn't, try being more conventional.
LOVE PARTNER 529; BUSINESS PARTNER 742

7 Some like to wander because they are restless. Others feel a need to escape. But some, like you, wander for the sheer enjoyment of it. You are one of life's genuine travelers.
LOVE PARTNER 521; BUSINESS PARTNER 743

8 Successful, obstinate, and very charming. What a curious mix you are. On the one hand, there is this difficult side; but on the other, you do seem to be getting your own way.
LOVE PARTNER 522; BUSINESS PARTNER 744

9 Difficult and dangerous, that's you. Everyone thinks you are a pussycat, but that's only because you are getting your own way right now.
LOVE PARTNER 523; BUSINESS PARTNER 745

BIRTH NUMBER

2

9

FULL NAME NUMBER

▲ David does not need your help to fight Goliath, Known Name Number 6.

YOUR UNIQUE PERSONALITY READING

A gentle soul you are, Birth Number 2, but you lack self-confidence. Sometimes you feel incapable of seeing a project through, so you don't. This failure shakes your confidence even further, and the vicious cycle continues. You shouldn't be so hard on yourself. Others admire you for having the courage to strive for your goals. Look to your inner personality, as expressed by your Known Name Number below, for strength.

KNOWN NAME NUMBER

1 You are ambitious and determined. You think you can get your own way pretty much all of the time—but you can't. You might need to be more diplomatic to achieve all you want to.
LOVE PARTNER 534; BUSINESS PARTNER 756

2 You are so charming it is dangerous. Is no one immune to your allure? It might be better if there were someone who could say no; getting everything you want isn't good for you.
LOVE PARTNER 535; BUSINESS PARTNER 757

3 You see the road ahead as straight and direct, and it might well be. But allow for detours—this will make you more interesting and less possessed.
LOVE PARTNER 536; BUSINESS PARTNER 758

4 You aren't always right, you know. You may have considered the possibility and rejected it on the grounds that it couldn't be so, but if you listened a bit more, you might learn something.
LOVE PARTNER 537; BUSINESS PARTNER 759

5 If you spent as much effort patching up your romantic relationships as you do on your friendships, you might gain more love and respect. You need to lay the groundwork.
LOVE PARTNER 538; BUSINESS PARTNER 751

6 What a bold little soul you are, always ready to take on the Goliaths of this world to protect the Davids. But do they really need protection or could they fire the slingshot?
LOVE PARTNER 539; BUSINESS PARTNER 752

7 Just because you have found the perfect way doesn't mean we all have to go the same route. Oh, I know it might be the right way, but please allow us to make our own mistakes.
LOVE PARTNER 531; BUSINESS PARTNER 753

8 Go on, dig in your heels a bit more. But perhaps you are standing in quicksand, and digging in your heels is a really bad idea.
LOVE PARTNER 532; BUSINESS PARTNER 754

9 Just because you have a good idea doesn't mean we all have to buy into it. It may not be suitable. It may be ahead of its time. Stop arguing and think of something else.
LOVE PARTNER 533; BUSINESS PARTNER 755

BIRTH NUMBER 3

FULL NAME NUMBER 1

> Like a bee buzzing busily from flower to flower, those with a Birth Number of 3 are usually hardworking and energetic. They can also be bossy and indifferent if they hurt the feelings of others.

YOUR UNIQUE PERSONALITY READING

The Birth Number 3 is characterized by success and completion in all spheres of life. You are a hard worker, and are driven to get the task at hand done—and done properly. You are seen by others as bright and honest, if a bit domineering and bossy, but you know that that's what it takes to get the job done sometimes. Your Known Name Number below can tell you what's really going on inside your head while you're busy acting professional.

KNOWN NAME NUMBER

1 You have a lot of drive and ambition; all you have to do now is to find a direction to channel all that energy into. It could be that this won't happen until later in life.
LOVE PARTNER 644; BUSINESS PARTNER 866

2 You are energetic, strong, and artistic, but you need to work with a very large canvas to achieve good results. Be careful not to get bogged down in the details.
LOVE PARTNER 645; BUSINESS PARTNER 867

3 You have a tremendous capacity to apply yourself, and you have the grit and determination to see things through. You can be a little too serious, though; learn to relax more.
LOVE PARTNER 646; BUSINESS PARTNER 868

4 You were sent here for a specific task, a purpose, a job. It's time you got on with it. You have been a rebel for too long now, and need to follow your true calling.
LOVE PARTNER 647; BUSINESS PARTNER 869

5 You have the drive and ambition, but may encounter setbacks. It could be that you have a misguided approach. Perhaps you need to appear more serious in order to impress others.
LOVE PARTNER 648; BUSINESS PARTNER 861

6 Others see you as a bit ruthless, but those who know you well know that you are very soft-hearted. You might do well to reveal this side of yourself to the people you meet.
LOVE PARTNER 649; BUSINESS PARTNER 862

7 You came here to achieve success, and you have the talent and energy to do so. What seems to hold you back is a restless spirit. Be content with what you have.
LOVE PARTNER 641; BUSINESS PARTNER 863

8 Outside the home you are well-liked and successful; but inside you tend to dominate a bit too much. Lighten up and relax.
LOVE PARTNER 642; BUSINESS PARTNER 864

9 Everything about you shouts determination and activity. You are so busy being busy you may well miss what it is you are attempting to achieve. Learn to see things from a distance.
LOVE PARTNER 643; BUSINESS PARTNER 865

BIRTH NUMBER THREE

73

BIRTH NUMBER 3

FULL NAME NUMBER 2

YOUR UNIQUE PERSONALITY READING

Those of you with a Birth Number of 3 are energetic and disciplined—we all know that we can depend on you to get the job done. That's okay with you—you like a challenge. You even seek out difficult situations to navigate, just to keep yourself on your toes. It's a good thing you are seen as charming, as your Full Name Number of 2 tells us, or else you might just inspire some envy. Your Known Name Number below tells the other half of the story.

KNOWN NAME NUMBER

1 Keep on plugging away with your ideas. You may well be light years ahead of your time, but the world will catch up eventually, and you will achieve considerable success.
LOVE PARTNER 654; BUSINESS PARTNER 876

2 It is okay to love and be loved. You don't have to remain quite so aloof from the rest of humanity. Come on and get involved with the rest of us. Deep down it is what you want.
LOVE PARTNER 655; BUSINESS PARTNER 877

3 By going your own way, you have achieved an awful lot, but there may come a time when you need a partner or two to help you. Time to learn how to work as part of a team.
LOVE PARTNER 656; BUSINESS PARTNER 878

4 If you work steadily at everything you have set your heart on, dividends will be paid. Maybe not tomorrow, but eventually. Don't lose heart and don't lose sight of your vision.
LOVE PARTNER 657; BUSINESS PARTNER 879

5 If you could settle down and concentrate on something—a new project, perhaps—you would benefit immensely. You aren't covering any new ground with your easygoing attitude.
LOVE PARTNER 658; BUSINESS PARTNER 871

6 You may find being out in the world a bit of a chore, but you have to get out of bed occasionally and search for fame and fortune. It will not come looking for you.
LOVE PARTNER 659; BUSINESS PARTNER 872

7 You don't need luck; you have talent and ambition. How did you end up with so many enviable qualities? The rest of us are jealous.
LOVE PARTNER 651; BUSINESS PARTNER 873

8 You sweetly and quietly go your own way, and couldn't give a hoot about the dictates of convention, public approval, or peer group pressure. Good for you.
LOVE PARTNER 652; BUSINESS PARTNER 874

9 Water will wear away a rock over time. You are relentless and determined, but you go about life in such a gentle way that people don't realize that you are as strong as steel.
LOVE PARTNER 653; BUSINESS PARTNER 875

BIRTH NUMBER 3

FULL NAME NUMBER 3

▲ It's time you faced your fears, Known Name Number 7.

YOUR UNIQUE PERSONALITY READING

Your Birth Number and Full Name Number are the same, which tells us that you are indeed how you seem to others: strong, enthusiastic, optimistic, and tenacious. The negative traits of the number 3—proud, controlling, and interfering—are also accentuated, however, so be careful, or you will make enemies. Your inner personality may show a different side of you altogether. Check your Known Name Number below to find out.

KNOWN NAME NUMBER

1 You have the talent, energy, and discipline to achieve anything you want. So why make such a fuss? We are all in awe of you. You don't need to tell us how brilliant you are.
LOVE PARTNER 664; BUSINESS PARTNER 886

2 Although you think you work best alone, this isn't really true. At some point you will need to learn to trust, and to take a partner on board. This may well be your soul mate.
LOVE PARTNER 665; BUSINESS PARTNER 887

3 You are everything we all yearn to be: successful, talented, well-disciplined, and energetic. We look up to you as a calm and well-ordered role model. Don't let us down.
LOVE PARTNER 666; BUSINESS PARTNER 888

4 Although you have a lot of talent and know where you are going, you also have a self-destruct button that you love to press just as it looks as if you are about to become successful.
LOVE PARTNER 667; BUSINESS PARTNER 889

5 If you delay getting on with your life any longer because you are too busy having fun,

you might forget what it was you set out to do. Don't lose sight of your goals.
LOVE PARTNER 668; BUSINESS PARTNER 881

6 Why do you always doubt yourself? You know what you want to achieve is right. The world is waiting, so go for it now. Be careful; procrastination is the thief of time.
LOVE PARTNER 669; BUSINESS PARTNER 882

7 It's time to take the plunge. Just take a deep breath, feel the fear—and do it anyway. You will have to jump in sooner or later.
LOVE PARTNER 661; BUSINESS PARTNER 883

8 You know you're right. We probably think you're right. So why argue? Just get on with it, and stop wasting your breath trying to convince us that you are right.
LOVE PARTNER 662; BUSINESS PARTNER 884

9 Every time you start out, you seem to get lost. Stop retracing your steps back to home base. You may flounder a little bit, but you will eventually see the light at the end of the tunnel.
LOVE PARTNER 663; BUSINESS PARTNER 885

BIRTH NUMBER 3

FULL NAME NUMBER 4

▲ Try to rediscover your sweet inner child, Known Name Number 4.

YOUR UNIQUE PERSONALITY READING

You do love to hear yourself speak, don't you, Birth Number 3? Your enormous reserves of energy are often spent chattering away, and it's apparent to all that you are brimming with self-confidence. We know from your Full Name Number of 4, however, that some see you as impatient and slightly opinionated. Your Known Name Number reading below can tell you a bit more about the real you.

KNOWN NAME NUMBER

1 You are a tower of strength. We all rely on you, and we all need you. That's fine, but you do need some comfort yourself, you know. If you don't learn to bend a little, you might break.
LOVE PARTNER 674; BUSINESS PARTNER 896

2 You are a rare creature—a thoroughly nice person. There is not a nasty bone in your body. You may be too good to be true—or just good at hiding the bad stuff. Which one is it?
LOVE PARTNER 675; BUSINESS PARTNER 897

3 You have a vision. You have the support and love you need to accomplish your dream. So what holds you back, apart from this impish need to provoke authority? Stop it right now.
LOVE PARTNER 676; BUSINESS PARTNER 898

4 As a child you were a little sweetheart—full of good intentions and charm. Something happened to make you resentful and hard. Find the cause and you will find the cure.
LOVE PARTNER 677; BUSINESS PARTNER 899

5 You're having a whale of a time, having fun and getting everything you want out of life.

Don't worry, the fun will continue for a long time to come. This is your enviable karma.
LOVE PARTNER 678; BUSINESS PARTNER 891

6 You devote a lot of time to your loved ones. Inside there is some resentment, though, as you would like more freedom. Wait a while and everything you want will come to you.
LOVE PARTNER 679; BUSINESS PARTNER 892

7 You have become trapped in a false world that simply isn't you. Break out now. This isn't what you set out to do and you know it. Listen to your intuition and go for your dream.
LOVE PARTNER 671; BUSINESS PARTNER 893

8 There is nothing you don't do first—set the pace, defy convention, and give us all a wake-up call. But why so rebellious? You have nothing to prove—you are already impressive.
LOVE PARTNER 672; BUSINESS PARTNER 894

9 You have all the qualities of a great leader and are simply outstanding in emergency situations. You don't lose control.
LOVE PARTNER 673; BUSINESS PARTNER 895

YOUR UNIQUE PERSONALITY READING

In ancient geometry, the number 3 is linked to the triangle, the symbol of logic, intellect, and reason. If 3 is your Birth Number, it may be fair to say that you are an inherently rational person, and are capable of making fair decisions. Your Full Name Number 5 tells you that others find you good company, and enjoy being around you. The Known Name Number reading below completes the picture of your personality.

KNOWN NAME NUMBER

1 Slow down and rest for a while. You will burn yourself out if you don't take a day off. I know you need to keep busy to maintain your success rate, but you can still chill out occasionally.
LOVE PARTNER 684; BUSINESS PARTNER 816

2 By staying ahead of the game, you are doing well. If you start napping, the rest of us might catch up. You are the hare; we are the tortoise. Keep moving—we're gaining on you.
LOVE PARTNER 685; BUSINESS PARTNER 817

3 There will come a time when you will need to settle down and find a partner—maybe even a job. Until then, enjoy yourself—that's the one thing you do superbly.
LOVE PARTNER 686; BUSINESS PARTNER 818

4 If there is a practical solution to the world's problems, you are talented and quick-thinking enough to come up with it. In the meantime, concentrate on matters closer to you.
LOVE PARTNER 687; BUSINESS PARTNER 819

5 You don't like being told what to do, nor do you like being given advice. But you might want to listen to someone very close to you—they know what they are talking about.
LOVE PARTNER 688; BUSINESS PARTNER 811

6 You have a gentle way of making your way through this world. You have an instinctive ability to know who to trust. Stay on the path that you are on and you will be just fine.
LOVE PARTNER 689; BUSINESS PARTNER 812

7 The world is a frightening, gray place, and you'd rather not be here. But you have to be here, so you must learn how to find light and color somehow. Try not to be so dreamy.
LOVE PARTNER 681; BUSINESS PARTNER 813

8 You are independent, entrepreneurial, and successful. But you are also difficult, bad-tempered, and rather controlling.
LOVE PARTNER 682; BUSINESS PARTNER 814

9 You have the discipline and the talent to be very successful. You also have the strength to upset the apple cart whenever you want to. Stop threatening, and either do it or back off.
LOVE PARTNER 683; BUSINESS PARTNER 815

BIRTH NUMBER

3

FULL NAME NUMBER

6

You like to be the one who comes to the rescue, Birth Number 3.

YOUR UNIQUE PERSONALITY READING

Typical of those with a Birth Number of 3, you enjoy a challenge, and love to be the one to come to the rescue when everyone is struggling with a problem. No wonder people see you as reliable and trustworthy, if a bit unrealistic in pursuit of your lofty goals. You shouldn't be surprised that people think this—after all, your Full Name Number is 6. It might all be an act, though; check your Known Name Number below to find out.

KNOWN NAME NUMBER

1 Everyone around you knows how reliable and strong you are—but they may well be leaning on you just a bit too much. Learn to say no and mean it or you will become drained.
LOVE PARTNER 694; BUSINESS PARTNER 826

2 Although you are successful and seem to have everything you want, there may be something missing from your life. Have you gotten bogged down in the daily grind?
LOVE PARTNER 695; BUSINESS PARTNER 827

3 You have a marvelous talent for taking care of others, and you seem to enjoy doing so. You may need to learn how to discharge all of that negative energy from others, though.
LOVE PARTNER 696; BUSINESS PARTNER 828

4 Sometimes we all have to compromise, if only to be able to work with others. This isn't giving in—it's being practical. You are efficient in every other respect.
LOVE PARTNER 697; BUSINESS PARTNER 829

5 Every time you feel the need to trust someone, do yourself a favor and allow yourself a bit of a cooling-off period. You don't have to say yes to everything immediately.
LOVE PARTNER 698; BUSINESS PARTNER 821

6 You have a great deal of energy, drive, and talent. They say it is being wasted on you, as you are too loving, too caring. Nonsense.
LOVE PARTNER 699; BUSINESS PARTNER 822

7 You have a natural talent for knowing what ails people. Use this talent well, and you will gain a reputation as a healer and counselor; use it unwisely, and people will see you as scheming.
LOVE PARTNER 691; BUSINESS PARTNER 823

8 Bide your time before you react. You have a knack for being slightly too honest and forthright. The world isn't ready for such truth, and you could wind up hurting others' feelings.
LOVE PARTNER 692; BUSINESS PARTNER 824

9 What a determined person you are. You don't give up. And why should you? Perhaps because you may be banging your head against a brick wall—but you may find a breakthrough.
LOVE PARTNER 693; BUSINESS PARTNER 825

YOUR UNIQUE PERSONALITY READING

No one knows better than you how hard you have worked for your success, Birth Number 3. With your agile mind, you are truly gifted at overcoming obstacles. We know from your Full Name Number 7 that others recognize you as a capable worker—that's why they always come to you for advice. But sometimes you wish that everyone would just leave you alone. Your Known Name Number reading below shows another side of your nature.

KNOWN NAME NUMBER

1 Inside you there is all this ambition, and yet you never seem able to get it out. Do you have the strength, but not the confidence? Try a different approach and see if things improve.
LOVE PARTNER 614; BUSINESS PARTNER 836

2 If you follow the same old boring formula that everyone else uses, you are destined for failure. The world is finally ready for the wacky, the strange, and the unorthodox.
LOVE PARTNER 615; BUSINESS PARTNER 837

3 You really must go your own way. You are being held back by other people's opinions. Be true to yourself and you will really fly; listen to others and you will be grounded.
LOVE PARTNER 616; BUSINESS PARTNER 838

4 You have an intuitive approach to life. If you combine this with your ability to be real and practical, you will enjoy great success. If you are unrealistic, however, you will not get very far.
LOVE PARTNER 617; BUSINESS PARTNER 839

5 It doesn't all have to be so serious. Although you want to help, you can still enjoy what you are doing without it affecting you adversely. Lighten up and be happy about what you do.
LOVE PARTNER 618; BUSINESS PARTNER 831

6 Just because you love people doesn't mean they have to do what you tell them. Let them go free. If they return, it was meant to be. If they don't, it just wasn't. That's all there is to it.
LOVE PARTNER 619; BUSINESS PARTNER 832

7 There is a nebulous energy inside you, a restless spirit that is trying hard to get out. Let it out. Don't worry about what others think. You need to be the real you in order to thrive.
LOVE PARTNER 611; BUSINESS PARTNER 833

8 You have always been individualistic and independent. This has stood you in good stead, even if things have been hard along the way. Hang on to your ideals; don't compromise.
LOVE PARTNER 612; BUSINESS PARTNER 834

9 Be aware that much of what you dabble in has great danger for you. You are not invincible. It's time to stop pushing your luck.
LOVE PARTNER 613; BUSINESS PARTNER 835

BIRTH NUMBER

3

FULL NAME NUMBER

8

▲ Find a spiritual system to believe in, Known Name Number 7.

YOUR UNIQUE PERSONALITY READING

People love working with you because you are enthusiastic, optimistic, and tenacious. The job will get done if it's given to you, Birth Number 3, no matter how busy you are. Others are tuned into your ability to focus and achieve your goals, and we know this because your Full Name Number is 8. But where does your drive and perseverance come from? Your Known Name Number reading below may provide a clue.

KNOWN NAME NUMBER

1 Why are you reading this? You already know that you are headed down the right path in life, and there is no doubt that you will reach your destination one day. Good for you.
LOVE PARTNER 624; BUSINESS PARTNER 846

2 Part of you wants to be charming and pleasant, while the other part insists on being rude and belligerent. Which side will win? The choice is yours.
LOVE PARTNER 625; BUSINESS PARTNER 847

3 You can't always make people do what you want. They have to decide for themselves, and if you badger them they will resent you. Stand back and give them room to breathe.
LOVE PARTNER 626; BUSINESS PARTNER 848

4 Does the word rebellious mean anything to you? Of course it does. It is your middle name. There is no authority on earth that impresses you, frightens you, or makes you obey.
LOVE PARTNER 627; BUSINESS PARTNER 849

5 You've been very lucky so far that no one has called your bluff. Can you keep it up? If you

let the mask slip, even once, you will be done for. Aren't you tired of this endless charade?
LOVE PARTNER 628; BUSINESS PARTNER 841

6 You will only achieve true success when you can look in the mirror and be proud of yourself and what you've accomplished. Be careful not to hurt those who love you the most.
LOVE PARTNER 629; BUSINESS PARTNER 842

7 You need to find a belief system to sustain you. You need something to nurture you during darker times, and it will have to be something pretty unorthodox to satisfy you.
LOVE PARTNER 621; BUSINESS PARTNER 843

8 You have the discipline for hard work and successful relationships. You may lack a certain flair for diplomacy, but you can work on that. You may also be a little too intense.
LOVE PARTNER 622; BUSINESS PARTNER 844

9 There is nothing that can stop you now. Hold on tight to your dream and don't let anything stand in your way. Believe in yourself.
LOVE PARTNER 623; BUSINESS PARTNER 845

YOUR UNIQUE PERSONALITY READING

Like most people with a Birth Number of 3, you may feel like a workhorse sometimes. But you wouldn't be so successful or wealthy if you didn't work so hard, right? From your Full Name Number 9, we know that others admire all the hard work you put into your charitable endeavors—and that the recipients really appreciate all you do for them. But there is more to you than this—look up your Known Name Number below to fill in the blanks.

KNOWN NAME NUMBER

1 You have the talent, the determination, and the strength to succeed. Follow your heart and stick to the truth. What more do you need? Oh, maybe a pat on the back. There, all done.
LOVE PARTNER 634; BUSINESS PARTNER 856

2 When you have something to say that means something to you, it might be best if you got someone else to say it. Otherwise, the message might get lost amid the mayhem that you cause.
LOVE PARTNER 635; BUSINESS PARTNER 857

3 What mysterious force drives you? You seem like such a nice person, and yet there is this dreadful need to take on the world. Back off and calm down. Breathe deeply. That's better.
LOVE PARTNER 636; BUSINESS PARTNER 858

4 As I walk through the valley, I think I would like to have you with me. Is there nothing that frightens you? Bold and courageous soul that you are, you are never afraid.
LOVE PARTNER 637; BUSINESS PARTNER 859

5 Your success in every aspect of life—career, family, romance—depends upon how much hard work you are prepared to put in. Very little? Well don't say you weren't warned.
LOVE PARTNER 638; BUSINESS PARTNER 851

6 You are determined and reliable. Stop prevaricating and follow your instincts. You may need to jettison some emotional baggage.
LOVE PARTNER 639; BUSINESS PARTNER 852

7 If you channel all of that incredible energy into caring for others, you will go far indeed. But first, you need to find a cause that you think is worth championing.
LOVE PARTNER 631; BUSINESS PARTNER 853

8 Go with the flow. You cannot turn the clock back, nor can you force the tide to turn around. Learn to float downstream and enjoy the journey—don't struggle against the current.
LOVE PARTNER 632; BUSINESS PARTNER 854

9 I won't upset you by telling you anything you don't want to hear—you are too volatile for that. But I would advise you to take time out before your pressure cooker blows sky high.
LOVE PARTNER 633; BUSINESS PARTNER 855

> ◀ Those with a Birth Number of 4 are usually the life and soul of the party. Hedonistic by nature, they attract others with their charm and enthusiasm for life, but they don't suffer fools gladly.

YOUR UNIQUE PERSONALITY READING

You know deep down that you can be bombastic and opinionated, Birth Number 4, but you also know that this is part of your immense charm. You are lively and great fun to be around. These innate characteristics are perfectly compatible with your Full Name Number of 1, which tells us that others also see you as the life of the party. But there is more to you than just fun and games. Your Known Name Number below can tell you what else there is.

KNOWN NAME NUMBER

1 You are a poor, driven soul, destined never to know any peace—that is, until you make it yourself, of course. You are a hurricane of creativity, talent, and drive.
LOVE PARTNER 744; BUSINESS PARTNER 966

2 You have the necessary strength, drive, and determination to express yourself forcefully and extremely well. You may, however, need to curb some of your excesses.
LOVE PARTNER 745; BUSINESS PARTNER 967

3 By going your own way and sticking to your guns, you have a good chance of arriving at your destination. Don't compromise, just be a bit more diplomatic. You know your own mind.
LOVE PARTNER 746; BUSINESS PARTNER 968

4 You are headstrong and determined, and you know what you want to achieve. Perhaps you haven't quite learned how to get there yet, but your time will come.
LOVE PARTNER 747; BUSINESS PARTNER 969

5 You are in great demand as an entertainer due to your enormous talent. You have

charisma, and are fun to be around. Watch that temper, though, and easy on the sarcasm.
LOVE PARTNER 748; BUSINESS PARTNER 961

6 You seem to have found a new way to motivate people, and are very good at getting others to look at problems in a new way. This is a marvelous talent.
LOVE PARTNER 749; BUSINESS PARTNER 962

7 No standard organized religion could ever hold any attraction for you. But a new cult? You may well become a founder or spiritual adviser of one. You don't mind rocking the boat.
LOVE PARTNER 741; BUSINESS PARTNER 963

8 There is an intensity that people can find scary. Lighten up a bit and allow people to see the friendlier side of your personality.
LOVE PARTNER 742; BUSINESS PARTNER 964

9 There is nothing you will allow to stand in your way in your furtive race to the top. You have the courage, determination, and energy to overcome all of the odds against you.
LOVE PARTNER 743; BUSINESS PARTNER 965

BIRTH NUMBER

4

2

FULL NAME NUMBER

▲ Aim for the moon in your search for a soul mate, Known Name Number 6.

YOUR UNIQUE PERSONALITY READING

Others can always rely on you, Birth Number 4, and you cherish this reputation for steadfastness. You would do anything in your power not to let others down. Others see you as sensitive and intuitive, as we know from your Full Name Number 2, and frequently come to you for advice, especially in the romance department. But you are more than just a shoulder to lean on. Your Known Name Number below can tell you how much more.

KNOWN NAME NUMBER

1 You have a wacky way of looking at the world, but it will lead you to success and to great wealth. Use your unconventional thinking patterns to supplement your creativity.
LOVE PARTNER 754; BUSINESS PARTNER 976

2 One day you will understand how to operate in this world; you will clap your hand to your forehead and say "of course, it's so simple." Until then, you are in a state of confusion.
LOVE PARTNER 755; BUSINESS PARTNER 977

3 Just when everything is going well for you, you do something to upset it all. You have this need to annoy others so that they withdraw their support. Next time, bite your tongue.
LOVE PARTNER 756; BUSINESS PARTNER 978

4 You are a charming revolutionary who manages to incite revolution with kindness and gentle words. You have a way of getting people to question the world around them.
LOVE PARTNER 757; BUSINESS PARTNER 979

5 You have a talent for working skillfully with your hands to create objects of great beauty

and usefulness. You might not yet recognize this talent, but you will soon—and everyone else.
LOVE PARTNER 758; BUSINESS PARTNER 971

6 When you find your soul mate, all of your dreams and goals will be fulfilled. He or she will have nothing to do with it; it's just that you will be happy enough to aim for the moon.
LOVE PARTNER 759; BUSINESS PARTNER 972

7 You are here to make us question things, but it seems you have forgotten about this task and have fallen asleep. Who will wake you up?
LOVE PARTNER 751; BUSINESS PARTNER 973

8 There is an entire section of humanity you have chosen to ignore. Why are you doing this? You are becoming isolated and reclusive, and are missing out on many things.
LOVE PARTNER 752; BUSINESS PARTNER 974

9 You seem determined to pick a fight. But who is brave enough to take you on? Perhaps only the universe itself. You are, of course, wasting your time.
LOVE PARTNER 753; BUSINESS PARTNER 975

BIRTH NUMBER 4

FULL NAME NUMBER 3

YOUR UNIQUE PERSONALITY READING

Nothing pleases you like a vacation to an exotic land, Birth Number 4. You are always up for an adventure, and value experiences far more than material possessions. Others recognize the free spirit in you—and how could they not? It oozes from every pore of your being! So your Full Name Number of 3 is in sync with your Birth Number. But there is still more to you to discover. Your Known Name Number below uncovers the rest.

KNOWN NAME NUMBER

1 You are steady, energetic, and strong. You work well, love deeply, and play hard. You are well-balanced, if not a little too driven. But you are fundamentally good and wholesome.
LOVE PARTNER 764; BUSINESS PARTNER 986

2 Rebellious, successful, and charming are you. If you are not working in the entertainment industry, then you should be. You have a lot of talent and creative drive.
LOVE PARTNER 765; BUSINESS PARTNER 987

3 Apart from your need to be in charge—in control of every situation—you seem fine, if a little bit intense and independent. Perhaps you feel there is no one who understands you.
LOVE PARTNER 766; BUSINESS PARTNER 988

4 Don't expect success too early in life. Remember, when you are young and outspoken, people call you a rebel. When you are older, people think you are a genius.
LOVE PARTNER 767; BUSINESS PARTNER 989

5 Pleasure seeking, rebellious, and independent—you lucky person. People

envy and admire your unconventional lifestyle, and many would willingly trade places.
LOVE PARTNER 768; BUSINESS PARTNER 981

6 You have a fascinating and unique way of caring about people, and have the rare ability to really listen when they speak to you. You should keep honing this wonderful talent.
LOVE PARTNER 769; BUSINESS PARTNER 982

7 Allow others to disagree with you. You may have found the right way for you, but it is only one way. There are many ways.
LOVE PARTNER 761; BUSINESS PARTNER 983

8 Independence and individuality can be desirable qualities, but not if you start a fight with anyone who doesn't agree with you. Stop being so defensive and be friendlier.
LOVE PARTNER 762; BUSINESS PARTNER 984

9 You have the drive to succeed, as well as the talent, energy, and enthusiasm. The only thing holding you back is the need to find fault with everyone else. Ease up a bit.
LOVE PARTNER 763; BUSINESS PARTNER 985

BIRTH NUMBER FOUR

YOUR UNIQUE PERSONALITY READING

Number 4 is the sign of the earth, and the term "earthy" couldn't describe you better. Both your Birth and Full Name numbers are 4, which makes you about as grounded as it gets. Reliable and steadfast is how you would describe yourself, and you can be sure that others would agree. But you are so much more than just the rock that centers everybody's world. Your Known Name Number below explains just how much more.

KNOWN NAME NUMBER

1 You are direct, assertive, and energetic. There is certainly no doubt that you know exactly where you are going, how to get there, and what you are going to do when you arrive.
LOVE PARTNER 774; BUSINESS PARTNER 996

2 You are an artist, a creative genius who seeks recognition for your fabulous work. You'll get it, but only when you present it differently. You need to be more tactful and diplomatic.
LOVE PARTNER 775; BUSINESS PARTNER 997

3 You are practical and enterprising. You are also independent, talented, and energetic. You seem to have found true happiness, and are content with your life.
LOVE PARTNER 776; BUSINESS PARTNER 998

4 You have just about all the stamina, drive, ambition, and energy anyone could possibly want. If you spend all that talent on yourself, you'll end up discontented. Spread it around.
LOVE PARTNER 777; BUSINESS PARTNER 999

5 All that energy and drive is being wasted. There's more to life than you think. You must have a goal to strive for, so choose one and go for it or you'll always regret it.
LOVE PARTNER 778; BUSINESS PARTNER 991

6 Deep down, you are soft-hearted, but you hide behind an "I couldn't care less" manner. It doesn't fool anyone, though.
LOVE PARTNER 779; BUSINESS PARTNER 992

7 You keep chancing your luck, and so far it has held out. But can it do so indefinitely? Knowing how audacious and crafty you are, the answer is probably yes.
LOVE PARTNER 771; BUSINESS PARTNER 993

8 You stand alone, head and shoulders above the present company you keep. The solution? Get a new set of comrades—find people who will understand and stimulate you.
LOVE PARTNER 772; BUSINESS PARTNER 994

9 The signals you send out scream "stay away!" Why is this? You have nothing to fear from us mortals. We only want to know and love you. Or is that the problem?
LOVE PARTNER 773; BUSINESS PARTNER 995

BIRTH NUMBER **4**

FULL NAME NUMBER **5**

▲ You are an incurable and unabashed romantic, Known Name Number 7.

YOUR UNIQUE PERSONALITY READING

You like spending time by yourself, Birth Number 4, but sometimes you feel like a hermit. You just need time alone periodically so that you can regroup and face the world again. You keep this private side of your nature to yourself most of the time, guarding it as you would a treasure. People know not to intrude, or so your Full Name Number of 5 suggests. Your Known Name Number reading below completes the mystery that is you.

KNOWN NAME NUMBER

1 You were born to be unconventional. You have achieved this in some measure, but you are still prey to what other people think. Time to go it alone and to stop worrying.
LOVE PARTNER 784; BUSINESS PARTNER 916

2 If you settled down and got on with work instead of wasting time on indulging all your passions, you could be very successful. Look to your dream and follow it through to completion.
LOVE PARTNER 785; BUSINESS PARTNER 917

3 You wasted a lot of time when you were younger, but you seem to have discovered the secret of industry and diligence. Good for you. Success awaits you sooner than you think.
LOVE PARTNER 786; BUSINESS PARTNER 918

4 Bless you. You work away steadily and relentlessly, without any sign of recognition or praise. You deserve a day or two off—and a pat on the back.
LOVE PARTNER 787; BUSINESS PARTNER 919

5 Just because you have the means to enjoy yourself doesn't mean you have to constantly throw parties. There is a season for fun and a season for hard work.
LOVE PARTNER 788; BUSINESS PARTNER 911

6 People rely on you, and you don't let them down. You accept responsibilities with a smile on your face and a song in your heart.
LOVE PARTNER 789; BUSINESS PARTNER 912

7 You wear your heart on your sleeve. You love to be in love—and to tell everyone about how wonderful it is. But is it ever as good as you think—and tell everyone—it is going to be?
LOVE PARTNER 781; BUSINESS PARTNER 913

8 You should learn how to take things a bit steadier, as you have very low energy levels at times. But you are always optimistic, and are eager to get on with the next project.
LOVE PARTNER 782; BUSINESS PARTNER 914

9 You can be persuasive, and would make an excellent politician if you didn't think such a job beneath your dignity. Oh yes, arrogance—another trait you have in abundance.
LOVE PARTNER 783; BUSINESS PARTNER 915

YOUR UNIQUE PERSONALITY READING

There is no more loyal friend than you, Birth Number 4. The trouble is, you don't always get the same degree of loyalty in return. You have been let down more than once, and it hurts. You can't help the way you are, though; soft-hearted and loving, you just can't turn away anyone in need, Full Name Number 6, and everyone knows it. But what you see isn't always what you get, as your Known Name Number reading below reveals.

KNOWN NAME NUMBER

1 Stubborn, strong-willed, self-reliant, determined, obstinate—you name it, you've been called it. You can't be enticed out of your position by anyone once you've taken a stand.
LOVE PARTNER 794; BUSINESS PARTNER 926

2 On the surface, you're very outgoing and confident; but underneath, you're a mass of complications and neuroses. You like going out, but not for long periods of time.
LOVE PARTNER 795; BUSINESS PARTNER 927

3 Those around you despair of ever seeing you sit down quietly for five minutes. You care deeply about those around you, but feel that none of this concern is ever returned.
LOVE PARTNER 796; BUSINESS PARTNER 928

4 If you don't allow a little time for yourself, you will suffer depression and stress-related disorders. Learn how to say no. Shut the door and spend some time alone recuperating.
LOVE PARTNER 797; BUSINESS PARTNER 929

5 You are compassionate, and are sensitive to the needs of others. Why can't you pay the same attention to your own needs? You can be moody due to the strain you put yourself under.
LOVE PARTNER 798; BUSINESS PARTNER 921

6 You have very expensive inclinations. You are well-adjusted, know who you are, know what you are doing, and know where you are going. You have an abundance of confidence.
LOVE PARTNER 799; BUSINESS PARTNER 922

7 You are volatile, explosive, and emotional. You have a great need to be loved, and can be very romantic. There is a stubborn side to you, but you can also be warmhearted.
LOVE PARTNER 791; BUSINESS PARTNER 923

8 There is something about you that is at odds with being in a romantic relationship. It could be that you simply refuse to compromise. Maybe it's best if you stay single.
LOVE PARTNER 792; BUSINESS PARTNER 924

9 You may fool most people around you, but there is a quivering heart, a deep passion lurking beneath your cool, businesslike exterior.
LOVE PARTNER 793; BUSINESS PARTNER 925

BIRTH NUMBER 4

FULL NAME NUMBER 7

▲ You flirt shamelessly, Known Name Number 7, but you're good at it.

YOUR UNIQUE PERSONALITY READING

Your ideal lifestyle is one of luxury and indulgence, Birth Number 4. Hedonistic to the core, nothing pleases you like a trip to a health spa or a meal at a fine restaurant. Thankfully, the image you project to others is more substantive; you come off as a spiritual, thoughtful person, Full Name Number 7, a good balance to your five-star desires. Your Known Name Number below completes the picture of your true personality.

KNOWN NAME NUMBER

1 Those around you, especially at work, think you are quick, efficient, and good at your job. You are, but under that coat of efficiency there is an untamed nakedness of lust and passion.
LOVE PARTNER 714; BUSINESS PARTNER 936

2 On the surface, you are very moral and decent; but if we were to strip away the veneer, we might find a darker, more devious soul who longs to be cruel and vindictive.
LOVE PARTNER 715; BUSINESS PARTNER 937

3 You do have a tendency to attract more lovers than any one person could safely handle, but somehow you seem to manage. Good for you, so long as you have the energy.
LOVE PARTNER 716; BUSINESS PARTNER 938

4 You are dramatic, creative, and a virtual tower of strength to those who work with you. You have real talent, as well as a flair for organization and for putting on a show.
LOVE PARTNER 717; BUSINESS PARTNER 939

5 You can be quite solitary when you want to be. This can lead to problems in relationships, as others may not understand your need for space and privacy.
LOVE PARTNER 718; BUSINESS PARTNER 931

6 You are fantastic at motivating a team. You will lead people to the very ends of the earth, and then make sure that they all get home safely.
LOVE PARTNER 719; BUSINESS PARTNER 932

7 You have inexhaustible energy and seem to be immune to sleep deprivation. You can be a bit intense sometimes, however, and need to learn how to sit back and relax a bit.
LOVE PARTNER 711; BUSINESS PARTNER 933

8 You find it hard to make any emotional commitments, but you still expect your partners to commit to you. You often surprise people with this double standard.
LOVE PARTNER 712; BUSINESS PARTNER 934

9 You can be extremely stubborn, and like things to be done your way. Your way may be the right way, but have you ever considered that it may not be? Of course not. Good for you.
LOVE PARTNER 713; BUSINESS PARTNER 935

BIRTH NUMBER FOUR

BIRTH NUMBER
4

FULL NAME NUMBER
8

YOUR UNIQUE PERSONALITY READING

Although you pretend to enjoy spending time with other people, Birth Number 4, the truth is that you'd rather be off on your own in an exotic locale. Trekking through mountains—solo, of course—is your ideal vacation. Your Full Name Number 8 tells us that others see this yearning for adventure as another one of your unconventional ways. Check the description of your Known Name Number for your inner personality reading.

KNOWN NAME NUMBER

1 You are a contrary soul with extreme mood swings and a nature that is hard to fathom. You are intuitive, and use this power unwisely at times. You can be demanding in relationships.
LOVE PARTNER 724; BUSINESS PARTNER 946

2 You are generous with your family, and enjoy giving them encouragement and support. If only you weren't so demanding. Don't put so much pressure on them.
LOVE PARTNER 725; BUSINESS PARTNER 947

3 You are not one of the world's great leaders (good, we don't need any more), but you are an original thinker. You can be a little bit too independent, but why shouldn't you be?
LOVE PARTNER 726; BUSINESS PARTNER 948

4 You are very good at research and are interested in a variety of subjects. You like to quote facts in conversation, and have a highly retentive memory for dates and statistics.
LOVE PARTNER 727; BUSINESS PARTNER 949

5 It isn't laziness that describes you. It's just that you always see a flaw in the plan at the last minute—too hot, too cold, too far, too expensive. Stop being critical and get on with it.
LOVE PARTNER 728; BUSINESS PARTNER 941

6 You are one of the smartest people around, but you cannot see where your own faults lie. It's time you admitted that you're not perfect.
LOVE PARTNER 729; BUSINESS PARTNER 942

7 You have an intuitive understanding of what people need to make their lives better— counseling, advice, help, support, and nurturing. People are precious to you.
LOVE PARTNER 721; BUSINESS PARTNER 943

8 You have limitless stamina, inexhaustible energy, and an adventurous nature that keeps you outdoors much of the time. The wilder the weather, the happier you are.
LOVE PARTNER 722; BUSINESS PARTNER 944

9 You have everything you need: charm, good looks, vivacity, intelligence, and lots of love—but there is still something that refuses to let you join in completely.
LOVE PARTNER 723; BUSINESS PARTNER 945

BIRTH NUMBER 4
FULL NAME NUMBER 9

▲ We need dreamers like you in the world, Known Name Number 3.

YOUR UNIQUE PERSONALITY READING

If you believe in something, you will defend it—a true sign of the Birth Number 4. You know this loyalty to ideas or views can be annoying at times, but you can't help yourself. Some people find you hard to take, but others find you brilliant and inspirational, as we know from your Full Name Number 9, especially given your talent at communicating your ideas. Your Known Name Number reading below can tell you more about yourself.

KNOWN NAME NUMBER

1 You are well-adjusted, good at organizing both other people and yourself, work well as part of a team, and are generally adept at solving problems, both long term and short term.
LOVE PARTNER 734; BUSINESS PARTNER 956

2 You are one heck of a tough negotiator, with a ruthless, dedicated streak. You work well within a team and are happy to take a back seat, but everyone knows where the real power lies.
LOVE PARTNER 735; BUSINESS PARTNER 957

3 The world needs dreamers like you, or we would all be too serious and materialistic. You are intuitively in touch with the heart and soul of humankind. You are also impractical.
LOVE PARTNER 736; BUSINESS PARTNER 958

4 You like egging others on to new and depraved experiences while you enjoy their discomfort and shame. You are the power behind the throne, but never the ruler yourself.
LOVE PARTNER 737; BUSINESS PARTNER 959

5 If you are not careful, your weaknesses will lead others astray. If the object of your lust

happens to be in a relationship—well, so be it. You are a romantic predator, and you know it.
LOVE PARTNER 738; BUSINESS PARTNER 951

6 You are a hard worker who enjoys being outside. You would like to combine your love of music with your love of horticulture.
LOVE PARTNER 739; BUSINESS PARTNER 952

7 You are popular; but most people are a little wary of you, and you don't make friends very easily. That said, there are a few people in your life who would do anything for you.
LOVE PARTNER 731; BUSINESS PARTNER 953

8 Whenever you feel settled and at peace, a tiny voice inside your head tells you that it is time to move on. Sometimes you want to shut the voice up, but you can't.
LOVE PARTNER 732; BUSINESS PARTNER 954

9 You have a lot to give the world and would probably be better off single. Not that this would ever happen, of course, as you need the dangerous cut and thrust of a relationship.
LOVE PARTNER 733; BUSINESS PARTNER 955

BIRTH NUMBER **5**

FULL NAME NUMBER **1**

Those with a Birth Number of 5 usually have great charm and are adept at all the social graces. They enjoy being around other people and can cheer everyone up with their presence.

YOUR UNIQUE PERSONALITY READING

You are a ray of sunshine in your friends' lives, Birth Number 5. With your wit and charm, people find you a real joy to be around. And you are certainly no recluse—others see you as someone who loves going out into the world and having fun, as we know from your Full Name Number of 1. But are you having as much fun deep down inside as you seem to be having on the outside? Your Known Name Number below may provide a clue.

KNOWN NAME NUMBER

1 You are a sensualist, a decadent pleasure seeker, and a creative and active hedonist. You seem to enjoy life a great deal, and are capable of entertaining both yourself and others.
LOVE PARTNER 844; BUSINESS PARTNER 166

2 You can be aloof, and might even be described as arrogant. You are superior and know it. You cannot fail to end up wealthy—unless you get caught and go to prison.
LOVE PARTNER 845; BUSINESS PARTNER 167

3 Make sure you earn a lot of money to cover your extravagance and generosity before you get into debt. You love entertaining, shopping, talking, and generally spending money.
LOVE PARTNER 846; BUSINESS PARTNER 168

4 You are an ideas person, always ready to move on to the next project. The question is, do you ever finish anything? You are easily bored and like to change everything constantly.
LOVE PARTNER 847; BUSINESS PARTNER 169

5 When you find your soul mate, you will settle down and be very happy. Once you discover your career niche, you will be successful and wealthy. It's only a matter of time.
LOVE PARTNER 848; BUSINESS PARTNER 161

6 You have enormous talent and energy, but don't like to take any credit, except for a job well done by a team. You are a very supportive manager who gets the best out of people.
LOVE PARTNER 849; BUSINESS PARTNER 162

7 You are talented and often in demand as a problem-solver. You have unlimited energy, and can wear out those around you.
LOVE PARTNER 841; BUSINESS PARTNER 163

8 An innovator you most certainly are. You are clever with your hands, and enjoy inventing new things. You have never been known to sit still or be at a loss for an idea.
LOVE PARTNER 842; BUSINESS PARTNER 164

9 You might take care of others around you a little better and treat them a little more kindly. You tend to set high standards and become agitated if people cannot meet them.
LOVE PARTNER 843; BUSINESS PARTNER 165

BIRTH NUMBER

5

2

FULL NAME NUMBER

YOUR UNIQUE PERSONALITY READING

You have an uncanny ability to cheer people up, Birth Number 5, and it hardly takes any effort at all! Maybe it's your wacky sense of humor, or maybe it's just your zest for life. You'll be happy to know, as your Full Name Number 2 tells us, that others recognize that you can be emotional and sensitive, and that you need cheering up sometimes too. Check your Known Name Number reading below to find out about your inner personality.

KNOWN NAME NUMBER

1 Your reputation for calling a spade a spade can make people hesitant about asking your advice, as they know that you will never dress up the truth with flattery or restraint.
LOVE PARTNER 854; BUSINESS PARTNER 176

2 You have a genuinely caring and responsive nature that enables you to work well with people without being needy. You can be a bit restless, and need lots of fresh air and exercise.
LOVE PARTNER 855; BUSINESS PARTNER 177

3 You are happiest working in the arts. You do need to concentrate a bit more and gaze out of the window a bit less, however, and you could do with being a bit more focused.
LOVE PARTNER 856; BUSINESS PARTNER 178

4 People like being around you, as you radiate fun and warmth. You love to entertain at home—dinner parties are your specialty. You have a passion for gambling—keep it in check.
LOVE PARTNER 857; BUSINESS PARTNER 179

5 You can be stubborn and a bit old-fashioned, but you can also be mellow and soppy when in love. You have a head for business and are creative both inside and outside the workplace.
LOVE PARTNER 858; BUSINESS PARTNER 171

6 You handle responsibility well, but it is often thrust upon you unwillingly. You don't let people down and are marvelous in a crisis. You seek harmony and hate discord of any sort.
LOVE PARTNER 859; BUSINESS PARTNER 172

7 You are loyal and faithful to ideas as well as to friends. You are robust and enjoy being outdoors. You can be jealous but are also kind.
LOVE PARTNER 851; BUSINESS PARTNER 173

8 You have a well-rounded personality and a sunny disposition. You typically wake up smiling and, if not upset about something, will maintain a cheerful frame of mind all day long.
LOVE PARTNER 852; BUSINESS PARTNER 174

9 You are a trustworthy, reliable person, and you cope well in emergencies. You are also very practical, and generally have no time to waste on what you would deem foolishness.
LOVE PARTNER 853; BUSINESS PARTNER 175

BIRTH NUMBER
5
3
FULL NAME NUMBER

▲ You are a born fighter with a fiery temper, Known Name Number 4.

YOUR UNIQUE PERSONALITY READING

Change is a key word for you, Birth Number 5. You will experience many changes in your life, but you will adapt easily to every one of them. You will never have any problem getting work if you change your living locale. Others see you as a hard worker, as your Full Name Number 3 tells us, so you will always be a valued employee. Your Known Name Number below can help you anticipate how you will react to all this change in your life.

KNOWN NAME NUMBER

1 You can be possessive and jealous—often with no good cause. These traits can drive people away, which is what you fear most. You are a sort of self-fulfilling prophecy.
LOVE PARTNER 864; BUSINESS PARTNER 186

2 The dilettante of the artistic world, that's what you are. You may be seen as lazy, but you spend so much time creating that you don't have any time left to do anything else.
LOVE PARTNER 865; BUSINESS PARTNER 187

3 You can be tenacious, and have great vision. You set a goal and then work steadily toward it. You may have inherited some of your father's temper, which can be volcanic.
LOVE PARTNER 866; BUSINESS PARTNER 188

4 You are a born fighter: quick-tempered and rebellious. As you grow older, you will learn tact and diplomacy. Until then, those around you expect fireworks—and get them.
LOVE PARTNER 867; BUSINESS PARTNER 189

5 You could sell ice cream to Inuits. You work hard and know how to spend the results of your endeavors. You are a party animal, but you are also up and working at the crack of dawn.
LOVE PARTNER 868; BUSINESS PARTNER 181

6 You are the great communicator of the numerology world. People listen to you—make sure what you say is worth listening to.
LOVE PARTNER 869; BUSINESS PARTNER 182

7 You have rare and mysterious magical powers —and you know it. Be careful to use these psychic abilities for good purposes lest they turn on you. You suffer from boredom.
LOVE PARTNER 861; BUSINESS PARTNER 183

8 The bull in the china shop—that's you. If you would only learn to control your impulsiveness and direct your energies more into team activities, you would fare much better.
LOVE PARTNER 862; BUSINESS PARTNER 184

9 Perhaps the world has grown too modern for such an old-fashioned character as you. You refuse to move with the times —and why not? You believe in truth, honesty, and justice.
LOVE PARTNER 863; BUSINESS PARTNER 185

BIRTH NUMBER

5

4

FULL NAME NUMBER

▲ You are very stylish, Known Name Number 5, but try not to be snobbish.

YOUR UNIQUE PERSONALITY READING

You are a smart one, Birth Number 5. You have a superior intellect and a gift for languages. For you, nothing beats a cup of coffee and a challenging puzzle. Others may see you as the nutty professor type, as we know from your Full Name Number of 4. You can be a bit of a slob, but that's because material possessions don't matter to you. But do these characteristics really define you? See your Known Name Number reading below and find out.

KNOWN NAME NUMBER

1 Constant and true—that's you. You allow the world to see the real you. Consequently, you are often surprised by how devious other people can be. You wear your heart on your sleeve.
LOVE PARTNER 874; BUSINESS PARTNER 196

2 You are strong, lively, and energetic—capable of exhausting those around you, but also capable of inspiring and motivating them. You have great stamina and can be resourceful.
LOVE PARTNER 875; BUSINESS PARTNER 197

3 You hate change of any sort, and can be seen as set in your ways because of this. This isn't necessarily the case; it's just that you like to be part of a tradition and a fixed set of values.
LOVE PARTNER 876; BUSINESS PARTNER 198

4 You aren't given to wild flights of fancy, daydreaming, or wanton longings. You prefer the safety of your fireside chair, where you can pontificate on the world and all of its ills.
LOVE PARTNER 877; BUSINESS PARTNER 199

5 You are stylish, educated, civilized, and refined. You are also a bit of a snob, and are proud of your breeding. Be careful, though, as you offend when you look down at "lesser folk."
LOVE PARTNER 878; BUSINESS PARTNER 191

6 You hate anything tacky or garish, and are discriminating when it comes to clothes, furniture, your house, your partners, and life in general. You adore the good things in life.
LOVE PARTNER 879; BUSINESS PARTNER 192

7 You are a sensualist and are in love with the best that life has to offer, from food to clothing to music. You admire beauty in art and literature, and have exclusive, exquisite taste.
LOVE PARTNER 871; BUSINESS PARTNER 193

8 The trappings of your life must be just right—homes, furnishings, cars, clothes, that sort of thing—or you will not be happy.
LOVE PARTNER 872; BUSINESS PARTNER 194

9 You have an inventive mind and are very clever. You are what might be termed an intellectual with strong opinions, and you have a forceful way of exploring the world around you.
LOVE PARTNER 873; BUSINESS PARTNER 195

BIRTH NUMBER 5

FULL NAME NUMBER 5

YOUR UNIQUE PERSONALITY READING

Both your Birth Number and your Full Name Number are 5, which means what people see is what they get. Luckily, what they get is pretty pleasing: you are a charming, witty, cheerful companion, and are much loved by all, except when your temper flares, as it can do sometimes. If people bothered to look past your happy-go-lucky exterior, though, they might see more. Your Known Name Number reading below can tell you what that is.

KNOWN NAME NUMBER

1 You retain a youthful approach to life— always inquisitive, always ready to learn, and always inventive. You adapt quickly and easily to new technology.
LOVE PARTNER 884; BUSINESS PARTNER 116

2 Speed is your motto, and you often devise ways to save time, cut corners, and generally save work. You like results to be quick and efficient, and bring fresh energy to any project.
LOVE PARTNER 885; BUSINESS PARTNER 117

3 You are a brilliant negotiator; you never let the other side see your potential until you have clinched the deal. This is why you are so successful in business—and so rich.
LOVE PARTNER 886; BUSINESS PARTNER 118

4 If you would stop talking for just a moment, you would realize that there is no one left in the room. You have a thirst for adventure and danger that frightens the rest of us.
LOVE PARTNER 887; BUSINESS PARTNER 119

5 You are always seeking the next adventure, the next safari, the next escapade. You are outstanding at recounting tales of your experiences, both orally and on paper.
LOVE PARTNER 888; BUSINESS PARTNER 111

6 You have a big heart that yearns for love and companionship rather than grand passion and lust. You have great personal charisma.
LOVE PARTNER 889; BUSINESS PARTNER 112

7 Privacy is important to you, and you can be quite shy and retiring at times. You are never at a loss for words, have limitless energy, and can keep going long after others drop.
LOVE PARTNER 881; BUSINESS PARTNER 113

8 You have a great talent for organization and make a good project co-ordinator. You can be a bit restless, and suffer from inner torment. You have a driving passion to change the world.
LOVE PARTNER 882; BUSINESS PARTNER 114

9 You like to have beauty around you and can be a bit snobbish about what you do. You tend to overrate your credentials; but what the heck, you have the charm to pull it off.
LOVE PARTNER 883; BUSINESS PARTNER 115

YOUR UNIQUE PERSONALITY READING

You love a good crossword puzzle, Birth Number 5—anything to exercise your agile mind! You like to be challenged mentally on a regular basis. You can be quite anxious, but hide this side of yourself well; others see you as a lover of harmony, beauty, and balance, as we know from your Full Name Number of 6. You keep other aspects of your inner personality well hidden. These are uncovered below in your Known Name Number reading.

KNOWN NAME NUMBER

1 Given enough time and trust, you can be as outgoing as the rest of us; it's just that you need to feel really secure and safe to venture forth. Once out, you are simply unstoppable.
LOVE PARTNER 894; BUSINESS PARTNER 126

2 You have many brilliant ideas, most of which involve making money by working from home. You may become successful and wealthy without venturing outside your front door.
LOVE PARTNER 895; BUSINESS PARTNER 127

3 You are a great lover of style. You enjoy perfect furniture arrangements and minimalist style. You can be found in large, clean, well-ordered white expanses of space.
LOVE PARTNER 896; BUSINESS PARTNER 128

4 You have a tendency to panic when faced with adversity, and don't cope very well with bills or money management. But then, souls like you shouldn't have to.
LOVE PARTNER 897; BUSINESS PARTNER 129

5 Some people accuse you of being a bit of a dilettante, as you have never done a hard day's work in your life. Luckily for you, you don't care much about what others think of you.
LOVE PARTNER 898; BUSINESS PARTNER 121

6 You are very caring and warm, and you love helping other people. Don't let your negative side surface, though, or you might be tempted to use your skills and knowledge for evil ends.
LOVE PARTNER 899; BUSINESS PARTNER 122

7 You are friendly and charming, and are good at putting people at ease. You treat your clients and friends as your family. Lucky them.
LOVE PARTNER 891; BUSINESS PARTNER 123

8 You are a true individual of extremes—all black and white rather than shades of gray—and you make the rest of us look pale by comparison. You have a big, bright personality.
LOVE PARTNER 892; BUSINESS PARTNER 124

9 What you want to do is rule. To be the most respected, the king or queen, the emperor, the Ultimate Ruler of the Universe. But let's be realistic; you may have to lower your sights.
LOVE PARTNER 893; BUSINESS PARTNER 125

BIRTH NUMBER 5
FULL NAME NUMBER 7

▲ Try not to drink your troubles away, Known Name Number 4.

YOUR UNIQUE PERSONALITY READING

You should watch your temper, Birth Number 5, or it may be your downfall one day. Luckily, you are quite cheerful most of the time, especially when you force yourself to relax and have some fun. Because your Full Name Number is 7, we know that others take your bad temper in their stride and chalk it up to eccentricity. But there is more going on in that formidable mind. Check your Known Name Number below to find out what that is.

KNOWN NAME NUMBER

1 You are very secure in yourself. You know where you are going and what you want to do. You are creative and talented. You have never suffered a moment's self-doubt in your life.
LOVE PARTNER 814; BUSINESS PARTNER 136

2 You have a sharp intelligence that borders on genius, and a natural ability to gather information and process it in a new way. Use this talent wisely and you will go far.
LOVE PARTNER 815; BUSINESS PARTNER 137

3 You are a flamboyant performance artist who likes to shock and horrify with your weird and wonderful tricks. You are larger than life, and have great charisma.
LOVE PARTNER 816; BUSINESS PARTNER 138

4 You are often broke, drunk, and out of love. But what the heck, at least you know you are alive, and those around you know they are alive too because you help them and motivate them.
LOVE PARTNER 817; BUSINESS PARTNER 139

5 You are intelligent and witty. Once you decide to change out of the somewhat tacky

costume you presently seem to delight in wearing, you will be a force to be reckoned with.
LOVE PARTNER 818; BUSINESS PARTNER 131

6 You are psychic and intuitive, interested in the soul and its fate, a lover of games and reading, and fond of hugging and group work. You are loyal and make a good friend.
LOVE PARTNER 819; BUSINESS PARTNER 132

7 You are never found at home if you can help it. You prefer to go out for fun, as your home is not really conducive to entertaining. You have a tenuous understanding of anything practical.
LOVE PARTNER 811; BUSINESS PARTNER 133

8 There is a touch of arrogance about you, but you will need this to succeed where you are going. You love being in the spotlight.
LOVE PARTNER 812; BUSINESS PARTNER 134

9 You can be quite cold when it comes to love. This comes from your perceived need to protect yourself from being hurt. Perhaps it's time to lower your guard and trust others again.
LOVE PARTNER 813; BUSINESS PARTNER 135

YOUR UNIQUE PERSONALITY READING

You are a master at correcting complicated situations, and have a real gift for overcoming adversity and bouncing back, Birth Number 5. Others see your ways as rebellious and unconventional, as we know from your Full Name Number of 8, but you know that there is no other way for you to be. You are just a natural troubleshooter. And there is more to you still. Your Known Name Number reading below reveals your inner identity.

KNOWN NAME NUMBER

1 You can be ruthless in your dealings with underlings, and have been known to be rude to waiters. You like old-fashioned standards. You may gain weight easily, but you carry it well.
LOVE PARTNER 824; BUSINESS PARTNER 146

2 Your greatest strength is the ability to see beyond the mundane, and you are able to pluck solutions out of the air that others would never have dreamed of. You are a real innovator.
LOVE PARTNER 825; BUSINESS PARTNER 147

3 You expect to be praised and loved. If anyone thinks bad things about you, they are subject to your disapproval, and you often hold a grudge. Perhaps you should lighten up.
LOVE PARTNER 826; BUSINESS PARTNER 148

4 You love exploring the darker recesses of the human soul, and experimenting with varied modes of spirituality. You are warm and funny, but can take yourself very seriously.
LOVE PARTNER 827; BUSINESS PARTNER 149

5 You can be emotionally needy, but if you receive a lot of reassurance, you are satisfied.

You can handle hard work, just so long as you don't have to talk to a lot of people.
LOVE PARTNER 828; BUSINESS PARTNER 141

6 You often display a remarkable aptitude for disguises. You like to change your personal appearance quite often.
LOVE PARTNER 829; BUSINESS PARTNER 142

7 You are always available, yet you are always in demand and are constantly busy. You like it like this, and can become miserable and sulky when you don't have enough to do.
LOVE PARTNER 821; BUSINESS PARTNER 143

8 You have a very easy way about you that impresses people, and they are likely to trust you. You are a good lover, although you do tend to pick partners who may be of some use to you.
LOVE PARTNER 822; BUSINESS PARTNER 144

9 You are motivated by money, but not by power or prestige. You like money for the comforts it can provide. It's lucky that you have the talent and drive to make lots of it.
LOVE PARTNER 823; BUSINESS PARTNER 145

BIRTH NUMBER **5**

FULL NAME NUMBER **9**

▲ You take very good care of yourself, Known Name Number 6, and it shows.

YOUR UNIQUE PERSONALITY READING

You need to be very careful not to find yourself stuck in a rut as this can be very dangerous for you, Birth Number 5. You do a good job of projecting a different you to the outside world, though: intense, energetic, and a lover of excitement is how others see you, as we know from your Full Name Number of 9. In all probability, the real you lies somewhere in between. See your Known Name Number below to find out more.

KNOWN NAME NUMBER

1 What you need is something solid to keep you organized. A decent laptop computer will do just fine. You take your work seriously, and don't have a lot of time for socializing.
LOVE PARTNER 834; BUSINESS PARTNER 156

2 Everything in your life is planned down to the very last detail. You hate surprises. You enjoy the cut and thrust of business and like it when negotiations go your way.
LOVE PARTNER 835; BUSINESS PARTNER 157

3 Although you have a very soft heart, you believe that people should make their own way in the world, and think that too much help makes people weak.
LOVE PARTNER 836; BUSINESS PARTNER 158

4 You are forceful, courageous and daring, reckless at times, and domineering. You will be a strong, proud leader in your chosen career—most likely as the head of a company.
LOVE PARTNER 837; BUSINESS PARTNER 159

5 You are independent, but might like to work more with a team to help you shoulder some of the responsibility. You have very refined taste, and can be a little old-fashioned and reactionary.
LOVE PARTNER 838; BUSINESS PARTNER 151

6 According to you, there is one rule for us and another for yourself. You are attractive and like to stay looking young and healthy. Looking successful and fit is important to you.
LOVE PARTNER 839; BUSINESS PARTNER 152

7 Stylish and attractive are words that describe you well. You are very much in demand as a raconteur. You love nothing better than to play the part of the amusing wit at dinner parties.
LOVE PARTNER 831; BUSINESS PARTNER 153

8 You are a mechanical genius, but you are also a grumpy nitpicker. You can be a bit taciturn, and haven't much time for entertainment.
LOVE PARTNER 832; BUSINESS PARTNER 154

9 You think life should be peaceful and full of beauty. You see no reason why you should have to look at the seamier side of life. Your existence is built around charm and elegance.
LOVE PARTNER 833; BUSINESS PARTNER 155

◀ A woman playing the sitar next to a garden pond, 1800s. Those with a Birth Number of 6 enjoy spending time at home and in their yard, as well as a love of music.

YOUR UNIQUE PERSONALITY READING

Those of you with a Birth Number of 6 tend to be reliable and trustworthy. Your idea of a perfect day is one spent peacefully at home, perhaps in your yard, relaxing and hanging out with your family. Others see you as honest and upright, as we can see from your Full Name Number of 1. But there are other, more complicated sides to you too. Look at your Known Name Number reading below to find out what these are.

KNOWN NAME NUMBER

1 You can be quick-tempered, impulsive, and impatient—you want everything now. You are also enthusiastic and generous, and very quick-thinking in emergencies.
LOVE PARTNER 944; BUSINESS PARTNER 266

2 You are not so hung up about looks; you are more concerned with principles, morals, and fortitude. You are practical and clever with your hands, and can fix almost anything in a pinch.
LOVE PARTNER 945; BUSINESS PARTNER 267

3 You can be conservative in your outlook, and aren't too ready to try new things; you prefer old, well-established ways and methods. You like to look ahead and to plan carefully.
LOVE PARTNER 946; BUSINESS PARTNER 268

4 When you have something to say you speak up, but you can be silent the rest of the time. You don't rush to conclusions. You are easily embarrassed and detest anything risqué.
LOVE PARTNER 947; BUSINESS PARTNER 269

5 You are a bit of a secret prude, and are prone to getting stuck in ruts. Friends know they can rely on you. You are slow to anger, but when you do blow, you do it in style.
LOVE PARTNER 948; BUSINESS PARTNER 261

6 You can be prone to clumsiness if you try to move quicker than you want to—which is usually quite slowly. Some see you as stubborn.
LOVE PARTNER 949; BUSINESS PARTNER 262

7 You are an old-fashioned lover who expects roles to be observed. The whole business of seduction and flirting is not for you. When you do fall in love, there will be a proper courtship.
LOVE PARTNER 941; BUSINESS PARTNER 263

8 You are an excellent judge of character, so you usually choose your partners well. When you do make a mistake, though, nobody can convince you of it.
LOVE PARTNER 942; BUSINESS PARTNER 264

9 You have great patience and are affectionate with your offspring. You aren't much for playing games, preferring a more educational approach; children will thrive under your care.
LOVE PARTNER 943; BUSINESS PARTNER 265

BIRTH NUMBER 6
FULL NAME NUMBER 2

▲ You love good food and are a great cook, Known Name Number 2.

YOUR UNIQUE PERSONALITY READING

The number 6 signifies harmony, beauty, balance, and perfection. Those of you with 6 as your Birth Number are attuned to each of these qualities, and they influence your life in significant ways. Other people see you as more concerned with emotions than actions, as we know from your Full Name Number of 2. This makes you seem sensitive and charming. Your Known Name Number below rounds out the full picture of your personality.

KNOWN NAME NUMBER

1 You tend to put on weight, owing to all that good food you like; but you carry it well. You are not great at expressing your emotions, but you can become depressed if you bottle them up.
LOVE PARTNER 954; BUSINESS PARTNER 276

2 Your love of good food knows no limits. You are an excellent cook and love to show off your culinary skills. The food you cook is heavy, filling, and traditional.
LOVE PARTNER 955; BUSINESS PARTNER 277

3 You have strong opinions that you will defend until the end—or until you decide to change them. You can be amusing and talkative, and have a great flair for languages.
LOVE PARTNER 956; BUSINESS PARTNER 278

4 You are a quick-thinking, independent sort of person who likes to be out in the world, wheeling and dealing and talking a lot. You can sell anything to anybody.
LOVE PARTNER 957; BUSINESS PARTNER 279

5 If you can't learn it instantly, you claim you don't want to know it. You don't like being

beaten by anything, but you also don't like to have to concentrate for too long.
LOVE PARTNER 958; BUSINESS PARTNER 271

6 You are a romantic idealist and expect your partner to be the same. You often get hurt in love affairs rather than the other person.
LOVE PARTNER 959; BUSINESS PARTNER 272

7 You expect everything to be perfect and are disappointed when it is not. Sometimes you don't think before you speak, and you find yourself promising more than you can deliver.
LOVE PARTNER 951; BUSINESS PARTNER 273

8 You have a drive and intensity that can be so focused and energetic that it can be scary. You are old-fashioned in that you equate sex with love and expect the same of your lover.
LOVE PARTNER 952; BUSINESS PARTNER 274

9 You are outstanding at getting information across quickly and succinctly. You talk fast, learn rapidly, and communicate extremely well. You are also very charismatic.
LOVE PARTNER 953; BUSINESS PARTNER 275

YOUR UNIQUE PERSONALITY READING

You are often accused of being too soft-hearted, Birth Number 6, but that's just the way you are—tough and cynical you are not. You project an energetic, disciplined image to others, as we know from your Full Name Number of 3, and everyone knows that you get things done. But you are a more complicated being than this. Check your Known Name Number below to get in touch with your hidden side.

KNOWN NAME NUMBER

1 You don't respond well to authority, so it is best if you work for yourself. The daily grind of an office will drive you mad, so get out there and sell your goods—it's what you're best at.
LOVE PARTNER 964; BUSINESS PARTNER 286

2 Like everything you do, your social life is frenetic and busy. The more activity and fast cars, fast foods, and fast adventures in your life, the happier you are.
LOVE PARTNER 965; BUSINESS PARTNER 287

3 Savings are not something you even think about—live for today, that's you. You'll be miserable in your old age if you don't put something away now.
LOVE PARTNER 966; BUSINESS PARTNER 288

4 You have a few really good friends, but friendships are something that let you down often. No one gives as much as you do and, consequently, you are sometimes hurt by others.
LOVE PARTNER 967; BUSINESS PARTNER 289

5 You suffer from a fear that you are missing something, and you are quite right. You rush everywhere and everything. In this way you miss a lot, as you are always between things.
LOVE PARTNER 968; BUSINESS PARTNER 281

6 You can be emotional and overly sensitive sometimes, but you are basically sympathetic and kind. You have a strong maternal instinct and a powerful imagination.
LOVE PARTNER 969; BUSINESS PARTNER 282

7 You love to dress comfortably—anything old and well-loved will do. You aren't a follower of fashion, but when you were younger, you may have gone through a period of rebellion.
LOVE PARTNER 961; BUSINESS PARTNER 283

8 You are shrewd and clever, with a strong intuitive power. You would make a very good counselor. You can, however, be a bit too sensitive, and will remember an insult forever.
LOVE PARTNER 962; BUSINESS PARTNER 284

9 You don't forgive very easily. You understand the emotions of others, and you use this for manipulative purposes. You are very possessive.
LOVE PARTNER 963; BUSINESS PARTNER 285

BIRTH NUMBER

6

FULL NAME NUMBER

4

▲ You expect love to last for all eternity, Known Name Number 3.

YOUR UNIQUE PERSONALITY READING

If there is a stray animal in the neighborhood it will find a home with you, Birth Number 6. You don't have the heart to refuse any living being in need, and often play the role of savior. This charitable aspect of your personality doesn't stop you from having a good time, however, and you love to indulge yourself; your Full Name Number of 4 tells us this. Check your Known Name Number below to find out what else you are capable of.

KNOWN NAME NUMBER

1 You love your family, and anyone else who loves them as much as you do. You are also fiercely protective of them. You don't like to be criticized or confronted by anyone.
LOVE PARTNER 974; BUSINESS PARTNER 296

2 You expect to be in charge, and can stifle relationships if you're not careful through your need to express your feelings in depth. Give your loved ones some room to breathe.
LOVE PARTNER 975; BUSINESS PARTNER 297

3 You are a great romantic and expect to fall in love forever at first sight, which you frequently do. You love to be wined and dined, and spoiled with presents and romantic outings.
LOVE PARTNER 976; BUSINESS PARTNER 298

4 If treated respectfully in love, you respond well and are a steadfast and faithful companion. If treated badly, you retreat into an emotional shell and won't come out again.
LOVE PARTNER 977; BUSINESS PARTNER 299

5 You shoulder responsibility well, and are an industrious employee. Any supervisor you

ever have will feel completely confident about leaving you on your own to complete a project.
LOVE PARTNER 978; BUSINESS PARTNER 291

6 As an employer, you are good at motivating your staff, although you set very high standards and take it personally if they are not met. You are happiest at home.
LOVE PARTNER 979; BUSINESS PARTNER 292

7 You like to look after your friends, and this means feeding them, buying presents for them, remembering them, phoning them, and being concerned with their health and welfare.
LOVE PARTNER 971; BUSINESS PARTNER 293

8 You are likely to put a lot of time into your home, and prefer to be there rather than out in the wide world.
LOVE PARTNER 972; BUSINESS PARTNER 294

9 You have a wonderful imagination, and can turn a hovel into a palace. You are neat to the point of obsession, though, and this can stop your friends from relaxing in your home.
LOVE PARTNER 973; BUSINESS PARTNER 295

YOUR UNIQUE PERSONALITY READING

Sometimes you have your head in the clouds, Birth Number 6. You mean so well and try so hard, but you are utterly unrealistic and impractical, especially in your quest to end poverty and suffering. Luckily, your earnestness is tempered by your sense of humor, and others just can't get enough—you really are the life of the party, Full Name Number 5. Yet there is more to you than meets the eye, as your Known Name Number below shows us.

KNOWN NAME NUMBER

1 You are creative and enthusiastic, energetic and positive. You are attention seeking at times, but you have the talent, charm, and personality to be at the forefront of most things.
LOVE PARTNER 984; BUSINESS PARTNER 216

2 You live off your charisma and charm, and the way you dress exudes these qualities. You are stylish, well-groomed, and sophisticated. People look to you for fashion tips.
LOVE PARTNER 985; BUSINESS PARTNER 217

3 You are among the most cheerful of people. You greet misfortune with open arms, as it gives you the opportunity to display your remarkable powers of recovery.
LOVE PARTNER 986; BUSINESS PARTNER 218

4 You are extremely generous with your time, hospitality, and friendships. You are trusting, and believe the best of people. However, you are quite gullible and easily fooled.
LOVE PARTNER 987; BUSINESS PARTNER 219

5 Your invariable knowledge of your own importance and strength of character can lead you to be a little smug and overly confident at times, and this can offend some people.
LOVE PARTNER 988; BUSINESS PARTNER 211

6 You have a sharp tongue and aren't afraid to speak your mind. You can be a little stubborn, and may need to lighten up a bit.
LOVE PARTNER 989; BUSINESS PARTNER 212

7 You like to start new projects, and exercise your considerable power in the business world. You prefer not to be alone, and seek out the company of other people.
LOVE PARTNER 981; BUSINESS PARTNER 213

8 Being in love is natural for you, and you never feel quite right without a partner. You are also an outrageous flirt, and this can cause problems with your current lover.
LOVE PARTNER 982; BUSINESS PARTNER 214

9 You are a great romantic, and you expect your partners to know this without telling them. As a result, your expectations in relationships are never quite realized.
LOVE PARTNER 983; BUSINESS PARTNER 215

YOUR UNIQUE PERSONALITY READING

You are a perfectionist, and value beauty above almost anything else. Because both your Birth Number and Full Name Number are 6, this aspect of your personality is quite strong, and is recognized by all who know you. You are also kind and loving, which saves you from being perceived as shallow. But there is still more to you waiting to be discovered. Check your Known Name Number below to find out about your hidden dimensions.

KNOWN NAME NUMBER

1 You have a great passion for music and dancing, and enjoy going out, partying, and generally staying up late and indulging to excess. You are one of life's great raconteurs.
LOVE PARTNER 994; BUSINESS PARTNER 226

2 Books and literature are beloved by you. Vacations can be exhausting for you—you try to cram so much into short periods of time, and they must have a serious element.
LOVE PARTNER 995; BUSINESS PARTNER 227

3 When you feel nurtured, loved, and cared for, your health is robust. If, however, you feel neglected or unloved, your nerves can become ragged and you may feel run down.
LOVE PARTNER 996; BUSINESS PARTNER 228

4 You have strict rules in your life and could be seen as fussy or critical; but, in reality, you are just setting standards for others to follow. You work hard and delight in constant activity.
LOVE PARTNER 997; BUSINESS PARTNER 229

5 Although you have an excellent fashion sense and are good with fabrics, your style is a bit severe and conservative, and might even be seen as a little old-fashioned at times.
LOVE PARTNER 998; BUSINESS PARTNER 221

6 You love to acquire knowledge and don't like having your experience questioned. You research carefully before making judgments and are usually right about most things.
LOVE PARTNER 999; BUSINESS PARTNER 222

7 You have no time for work-shy people. You are responsive on a physical level, but may be seen as emotionally detached. You are witty and have a sophisticated, quick sense of humor.
LOVE PARTNER 991; BUSINESS PARTNER 223

8 You are extremely physically responsive, but may be seen as slightly cold. You love a good joke. You can be quite cruel in your criticisms.
LOVE PARTNER 992; BUSINESS PARTNER 224

9 You fall in love with quiet dignity and are really searching for companionship. You look for partners to whom you can be devoted and for whom you have great respect.
LOVE PARTNER 993; BUSINESS PARTNER 225

BIRTH NUMBER
6

7
FULL NAME NUMBER

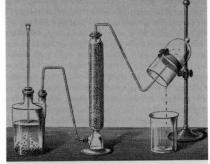

▲ Your intellect would be put to good use in science, Known Name Number 3.

YOUR UNIQUE PERSONALITY READING

As a Birth Number 6, you feel like you make sacrifices for everyone else and get nothing in return. Perhaps you should lose the martyr complex and start standing up for yourself. Although you may not realize it, people do look up to you—we know this from your Full Name Number of 7. Perhaps there are other parts of yourself with which you need to get acquainted. Check your Known Name Number to find out what these may be.

KNOWN NAME NUMBER

1 You are not one of life's great romantics and may actually shy away from any overt display of romance. You believe we should all keep our personal feelings to ourselves.
LOVE PARTNER 914; BUSINESS PARTNER 236

2 You fear criticism and will become withdrawn if you feel insecure. You like to try new things, and are more adventurous than others think. You are a voracious reader.
LOVE PARTNER 915; BUSINESS PARTNER 237

3 Because of your ability to pay attention to detail, you are good at processing information—information technology or scientific research would be good jobs for you.
LOVE PARTNER 916; BUSINESS PARTNER 238

4 You need your friends to hold the same sort of views as you, and you don't really like unconventional types. You like your friends to be refined, educated, and not too emotional.
LOVE PARTNER 917; BUSINESS PARTNER 239

5 You like an easygoing life. You may be seen as frivolous because you back away from unpleasantness; but you are refined and elegant, and don't need confusion around you.
LOVE PARTNER 918; BUSINESS PARTNER 231

6 You are fairly decisive most of the time. It's true you may change your mind seconds later, but as soon as you know what it is that you want, you're totally convinced.
LOVE PARTNER 919; BUSINESS PARTNER 232

7 You are co-operative and helpful, and will go out of your way to assist friends in need. You have a formidable intellect, and would make a good teacher.
LOVE PARTNER 911; BUSINESS PARTNER 233

8 You have strong beliefs and communicate them well. You are warm, loving, and have great taste. You would make a good diplomat because you can see both points of view.
LOVE PARTNER 912; BUSINESS PARTNER 234

9 Loud people annoy you. You detest arguments, unless they're of the intellectual variety, in which case you can't get enough.
LOVE PARTNER 913; BUSINESS PARTNER 235

BIRTH NUMBER

6

8

FULL NAME NUMBER

YOUR UNIQUE PERSONALITY READING

You are an inherently good person, Birth Number 6. You love helping others, and have a gentle nature. You believe it is your duty to care for those in need, but perhaps you shouldn't put such stress on yourself. Maybe it's because others perceive you as such a capable leader, as we know from your Full Name Number of 8, that you always end up leading the troops. Perhaps your Known Name Number below can teach you more about yourself.

KNOWN NAME NUMBER

1 You enjoy being admired for your strength of character and wackiness, although a lot of it is done for effect—and you know it. You simply hate being hurried or told to change.
LOVE PARTNER 924; BUSINESS PARTNER 246

2 In public life, you may appear casual, but you are actually a stickler for tradition. This laissez-faire attitude of yours is all contrived; you are actually quite a traditionalist.
LOVE PARTNER 925; BUSINESS PARTNER 247

3 You are industrious on the job, but you take ages to do anything. You communicate well, and that's what you do best: chatting, as others call it. You have a reputation at work as a slacker.
LOVE PARTNER 926; BUSINESS PARTNER 248

4 You are immensely friendly at work and very popular, although you probably don't think you are. You are a great one for trade unions and know your rights. You hate injustice.
LOVE PARTNER 927; BUSINESS PARTNER 249

5 The ideal occupations for you involve three key ingredients: communication, beauty, and the ability to make business deals. Get these factors right and you will be happy in your job.
LOVE PARTNER 928; BUSINESS PARTNER 241

6 You don't like loud, uncouth people, and you expect your friends to be well-groomed, sophisticated, and well-read. You love discussing books, music, and the theater.
LOVE PARTNER 929; BUSINESS PARTNER 242

7 You are quite a social creature, and can get depressed if you spend too much time on your own. You recover quickly from physical illness but you need more fresh air.
LOVE PARTNER 921; BUSINESS PARTNER 243

8 You are in control of yourself and are quite determined. You know what you want, how to get it, and what to do once you've got it.
LOVE PARTNER 922; BUSINESS PARTNER 244

9 You don't have any weaknesses—or at least none that you can see. You believe in strength and purpose, and can't abide laziness, secrets being hidden from you, or being ignored.
LOVE PARTNER 923; BUSINESS PARTNER 245

PERSONALITY GUIDE

BIRTH NUMBER

6

9

FULL NAME NUMBER

▲ You rely on astrological readings to guide you, Known Name Number 7.

YOUR UNIQUE PERSONALITY READING

You are used to getting all sorts of amorous attention, attractive person that you are, Birth Number 6. Just be careful not to let it go to your head. Others see you as more than just a pretty face, however—they see you as imaginative, sensitive, and intuitive, all of which you are. But there is still more to be found behind that marvelous exterior; your Known Name Number below can help you uncover what else it is about you that is so attractive.

KNOWN NAME NUMBER

1 You don't like trusting people, especially strangers, yet you expect to be trusted yourself. You think that the means justifies the end, and so others may think you devious.
LOVE PARTNER 934; BUSINESS PARTNER 256

2 You feel love intensely and can become quite dependent on your loved ones—not that they'd ever be allowed to know it. You don't like showing your emotions and can seem remote.
LOVE PARTNER 935; BUSINESS PARTNER 257

3 You like to be in charge in a relationship. You're not particularly romantic, but can be quite tender when you want to be. You come across as being embarrassed to be in love.
LOVE PARTNER 936; BUSINESS PARTNER 258

4 You work hard and expect others to do so as well, and you can appear ruthless in your need to get a job done. You are good at solving problems. You don't expect to fail, and rarely do.
LOVE PARTNER 937; BUSINESS PARTNER 259

5 You can process information effortlessly and make quantum leaps that others can only guess at. Because of this shrewd ability, you can see into the very depths of the souls of others.
LOVE PARTNER 938; BUSINESS PARTNER 251

6 You are good to your friends and always lend them a shoulder to cry on. They think you are kind, but all you really want to know is their secrets. You are a generous person.
LOVE PARTNER 939; BUSINESS PARTNER 252

7 Your interests invariably concern discovery. You like detective stories, research, and mysteries. You probably have a large library of books on the occult and esoteric subjects.
LOVE PARTNER 931; BUSINESS PARTNER 253

8 You are a wise, responsible person. You value your freedom highly, and don't like rules or routine. You seek truth above all things.
LOVE PARTNER 932; BUSINESS PARTNER 254

9 You don't like making promises—you know you'll break them—and you simply hate being disapproved of. You resent being accused of dishonesty; you take this as a personal affront.
LOVE PARTNER 933; BUSINESS PARTNER 255

BIRTH NUMBER
7

FULL NAME NUMBER
1

A Tibetan magic square used for divination. Those with a Birth Number of 7 are usually spiritual, sensitive, intuitive, and even psychic, with an interest in mysticism.

YOUR UNIQUE PERSONALITY READING

With a Birth Number of 7, you can be extremely intuitive—even psychic. You are also a sensitive, spiritual soul, and are prone to philosophical thoughts. Others see you as confident and capable, as is evident from your Full Name Number of 1, as well as straightforward and bright. Your Known Name Number may tell a completely different story, though; check yours below to find out about your true identity.

KNOWN NAME NUMBER

1 You have drive and a relentless ambition that propels you to the top without anyone ever realizing you were aiming there. You have a cheerful optimism usually lacking in a high flier.
LOVE PARTNER 144; BUSINESS PARTNER 366

2 If more people had your approach and were less demanding, this world would be a more pleasant place. You are always ready to lend a hand to anyone also on their way up.
LOVE PARTNER 145; BUSINESS PARTNER 367

3 You are loyal to your ideals and to your partners. When you fall in love, you will stay there for the rest of your life. You are a thoroughly nice person.
LOVE PARTNER 146; BUSINESS PARTNER 368

4 You can be outspoken and don't pull any punches when you have to speak your mind. You don't like being crossed, rejected, ignored, given the runaround, or criticized.
LOVE PARTNER 147; BUSINESS PARTNER 369

5 You like honesty, activity, and travel (including mental journeys). You are also an idealistic, optimistic, cheerful soul who likes to generate new ideas and to be constantly busy.
LOVE PARTNER 148; BUSINESS PARTNER 361

6 You set your sights very high, not only for yourself but for the whole of humanity, with whom you feel an intense personal affinity. You are a visionary, a poet, and a dreamer.
LOVE PARTNER 149; BUSINESS PARTNER 362

7 You are a philosopher and an intellectual. You love to dream, have visions and goals, and yearn to make this world a better place.
LOVE PARTNER 141; BUSINESS PARTNER 363

8 You sincerely believe that you will be successful—if not today, then tomorrow. You remain cheerful no matter what life throws your way, and pick yourself up from adversity quickly.
LOVE PARTNER 142; BUSINESS PARTNER 364

9 You are so easygoing that you are too gullible, too easy to lead astray. You can also be untidy and disorganized, and are not very punctual. You usually forget anniversaries.
LOVE PARTNER 143; BUSINESS PARTNER 365

BIRTH NUMBER SEVEN

BIRTH NUMBER
7
FULL NAME NUMBER
2

▲ You really come alive when traveling, Birth Number 7.

YOUR UNIQUE PERSONALITY READING

Travel is very important to those with a Birth Number of 7. The only time they feel truly alive is when they are on a journey—be it to the nearby countryside, or to a place far away. For those who fit this bill, your Full Name Number of 2 tells us that there are people who view your tendency to disappear from life as evidence that you hide from responsibilities. Check your Known Name Number below to discover another side of the real you.

KNOWN NAME NUMBER

1 Some people like a challenge, but you like to wrestle life to the ground, beat it up, and then spit it out. You like to be in charge, and can be difficult when you don't get your way.
LOVE PARTNER 154; BUSINESS PARTNER 376

2 You are impulsive and can be reckless, which sometimes necessitates you backing out of a hole you have dug for yourself. You know the old adage: when you're in a hole, stop digging.
LOVE PARTNER 155; BUSINESS PARTNER 377

3 You are optimistic, daring, outspoken, and cheerful. You inspire us and make us want to be as bright, loud, and exuberant as you. You can push it, though, and be a bit overbearing.
LOVE PARTNER 156; BUSINESS PARTNER 378

4 You can be impatient in general and are often slipshod at work, but your charm and delightful personality always gets you out of trouble. You have a devil-may-care attitude.
LOVE PARTNER 157; BUSINESS PARTNER 379

5 You can be a bit of a rake, but are often forgiven because you are so charming, so

refined, and so in control that people trust you. If you are doing it, they think it can't be wrong.
LOVE PARTNER 158; BUSINESS PARTNER 371

6 If anyone is going to discover the missing link, it will be you. If anyone is going to invent a new rocket fuel, it will be you. You are always on the cutting edge.
LOVE PARTNER 159; BUSINESS PARTNER 372

7 You can be quick-tempered, impulsive, and impatient. However, you are also enthusiastic, kind-hearted, and quick-thinking.
LOVE PARTNER 151; BUSINESS PARTNER 373

8 You like to be in charge and setting the agenda. You are relentlessly energetic and optimistic, and are such a force to be reckoned with that others may see you as domineering.
LOVE PARTNER 152; BUSINESS PARTNER 374

9 You have such enthusiasm for life that nothing holds you back for long. You see any setbacks as challenges, and you have the ability to recover quickly from disasters.
LOVE PARTNER 153; BUSINESS PARTNER 375

YOUR UNIQUE PERSONALITY READING

You have a very deep inner life that you manage to keep hidden from pretty well everyone. Nobody knows the real you—how can they, when you won't let anyone in, Birth Number 7? Energetic, disciplined, and organized on the outside—a typical Full Name Number 3— you never let on that all sorts of turmoil is buzzing around inside of you. What other mysteries are you hiding? Your Known Name Number reading below tells us.

KNOWN NAME NUMBER

1 You are spiritual, energetic, and strong. Because you fight our causes for us, we will follow you wherever you go. You are our savior, our leader, our hero. We look up to you.
LOVE PARTNER 164; BUSINESS PARTNER 386

2 You are open and honest in your dealings with others and expect them to be the same with you. These expectations can sometimes lead to hurt and disappointment.
LOVE PARTNER 165; BUSINESS PARTNER 387

3 You like to take risks and seem to lead a charmed life. You are relentless in your pursuit of your aspirations and will continue trying long after others have given up.
LOVE PARTNER 166; BUSINESS PARTNER 388

4 You like to be adored and in love. You enjoy being seduced and feel unhappy without a love interest in your life. You quickly get bored, though, and must have new projects on the go.
LOVE PARTNER 167; BUSINESS PARTNER 389

5 You adore good food and wine, enjoy travel and adventure, and hate routine. You would like to have lots of money, but only for the things it can buy—not for the prestige.
LOVE PARTNER 168; BUSINESS PARTNER 381

6 You are an initiator of new ideas and new projects. You will do well in any occupation where this inventive spirit is allowed to flourish. You will not be successful if you feel bored.
LOVE PARTNER 169; BUSINESS PARTNER 382

7 You are creative, with strong ideas that cry out for expression. You hate rules, discipline, and petty tyrants. You will thrive if given the opportunity to run your own creative business.
LOVE PARTNER 161; BUSINESS PARTNER 383

8 You are not a great one for relaxing; you prefer to have something to do. When left unattended you get bored—and into trouble.
LOVE PARTNER 162; BUSINESS PARTNER 384

9 You like parties and enjoy being the life and soul of them. You enjoy themed occasions, especially when you can get dressed up and be outrageous. You are a fun-loving dilettante.
LOVE PARTNER 163; BUSINESS PARTNER 385

BIRTH NUMBER

7

4

FULL NAME NUMBER

YOUR UNIQUE PERSONALITY READING

As a Birth Number 7, you are the sage that everyone else comes to for help and advice. Others have complete faith in you, and you are good at this role. Perhaps they look up to you so because they see you as practical and reliable—at least that's what your Full Name Number 4 tells us. But there are other sides to you that are just as fascinating. Your inner personality is revealed below in your Known Name Number reading.

KNOWN NAME NUMBER

1 You love socializing and being in the thick of things. You are the type of person who likes to use friends and social contacts for business deals and money-making ventures.
LOVE PARTNER 174; BUSINESS PARTNER 396

2 You are quick, lively, and very much on the ball. You love looking for opportunities, especially to increase your wealth. You have immense self-control and hide your emotions.
LOVE PARTNER 175; BUSINESS PARTNER 397

3 For you, family is probably more important than anything else. You are a great provider, and regard it as your duty to make sure your family wants for nothing.
LOVE PARTNER 176; BUSINESS PARTNER 398

4 You have tremendous sex appeal, and it is through sex that you find your true identity. With you there is no game playing or nonsense—just good old-fashioned sex.
LOVE PARTNER 177; BUSINESS PARTNER 399

5 You need a partner who is as lively as you, or you're inclined to get bored. If your partner doesn't stimulate you sufficiently, you would have no qualms about taking a new lover.
LOVE PARTNER 178; BUSINESS PARTNER 391

6 You have the unique ability to be able to see which parts of an issue are important and which are irrelevant. Whatever you do, make sure you that you put this talent to good use.
LOVE PARTNER 179; BUSINESS PARTNER 392

7 You have quite a reputation for being good at making money. You are an innovator, and are always ready to rise to a challenge.
LOVE PARTNER 171; BUSINESS PARTNER 393

8 Although you may be known for your daring, you rarely take risks, preferring instead to have worked out the odds well in advance—otherwise, you simply walk away.
LOVE PARTNER 172; BUSINESS PARTNER 394

9 You make a better boss than an underling, although you get bogged down in routine easily. You are better at igniting projects than at seeing them through.
LOVE PARTNER 173; BUSINESS PARTNER 395

PERSONALITY GUIDE

BIRTH NUMBER **7**
FULL NAME NUMBER **5**

▲ You are happiest working outdoors, Known Name Number 8.

YOUR UNIQUE PERSONALITY READING

Just accept the fact that everyone values your opinion. People are never going to stop coming to you for advice, Birth Number 7, so stop resenting the intrusions into your time. And it's not just your advice that people seek—it's also your charming company, as your Full Name Number of 5 tells us. So be flattered that so many think you so wise. Check your Known Name Number below for more insight into your inner personality.

KNOWN NAME NUMBER

1 You are at your best in any occupation or career that allows you to develop your abilities, such as directing, administrating, or managing. You are lively and full of ideas.
LOVE PARTNER 184; BUSINESS PARTNER 316

2 You have a knack for putting people at ease with your cheerful, outgoing, and warm personality. You do have a tendency to talk too much, though, particularly about yourself.
LOVE PARTNER 185; BUSINESS PARTNER 317

3 You are known for your loyalty, and will stick by your friends no matter what. You are also very nonjudgmental. You are very kind, which is why people like you so much.
LOVE PARTNER 186; BUSINESS PARTNER 318

4 You are a formidable character. You are set in your ways and have definite opinions, all of which may seem a little old-fashioned to others. You are tenacious and like to work hard.
LOVE PARTNER 187; BUSINESS PARTNER 319

5 People know they can rely on you for just about anything. You get the job done, and

are a sensible person. You have been known to hop off the tracks occasionally—but who hasn't?
LOVE PARTNER 188; BUSINESS PARTNER 311

6 You like everyone around you, especially your family, to adhere to the same values of morality, tradition, and discipline as you do. When they fail to do so, you find it hard to cope.
LOVE PARTNER 189; BUSINESS PARTNER 312

7 You see everything at face value, and believe that everyone else is as honest as you are. Well, we're not. Is that a shock?
LOVE PARTNER 181; BUSINESS PARTNER 313

8 In any job, you bring the same methodical, relentless spirit you do to everything in life. You don't mind a bit of fresh air or rain. This makes you ideally suited to working outdoors.
LOVE PARTNER 182; BUSINESS PARTNER 314

9 You don't like to take breaks, to be seen as lazy, or to be seen enjoying life too much. Whatever you do for a living, your goal is to achieve security and a good pension plan.
LOVE PARTNER 183; BUSINESS PARTNER 315

BIRTH NUMBER

7

FULL NAME NUMBER

6

You believe in peace and harmony,
Known Name Number 6.

YOUR UNIQUE PERSONALITY READING

Do you ever feel like you understand situations that you should really know nothing about? Do you often know what's going to happen before it happens? If so, this is no surprise; people with a Birth Number of 7 can be extremely psychic. Others see you as a sensual being, which, of course, you are as well. You keep the real you hidden, though. You may find that your Known Name Number below gives away some of your secret.

KNOWN NAME NUMBER

1 You don't like making promises—you know you'll break them, and you simply hate being disapproved of. You are an honest person, and you can hold a grudge for a long time.
LOVE PARTNER 194; BUSINESS PARTNER 326

2 You are honest and loyal. Ideally, you will have a career in one of the caring professions because your cheerful disposition will enable you to get through a hard day.
LOVE PARTNER 195; BUSINESS PARTNER 327

3 You can be a little outspoken. If you're not careful, that loose tongue of yours will get you into trouble. You always spring to the defense of the underdog.
LOVE PARTNER 196; BUSINESS PARTNER 328

4 You are reliable, dependable, and don't panic in a crisis. You like to speak when you have something to say, but can be silent the rest of the time. You don't rush to conclusions.
LOVE PARTNER 197; BUSINESS PARTNER 329

5 You don't like it when fun is made at your expense. Perhaps you should lighten up. You

are slow to anger; but when you do blow, you do it in style. You can be prone to clumsiness.
LOVE PARTNER 198; BUSINESS PARTNER 321

6 You don't like to feel too safe and enjoy risk, challenge, and adventure. You are not a great one for paperwork, rules, or authority. You are a free spirit looking for peace and harmony.
LOVE PARTNER 199; BUSINESS PARTNER 322

7 Because you can read people well, the partners that you choose are usually right for you. If you do make a mistake, you will never admit that you were wrong.
LOVE PARTNER 191; BUSINESS PARTNER 323

8 You enjoy the company of people who have, like you, good taste. You don't like your friends to be too emotional.
LOVE PARTNER 192; BUSINESS PARTNER 324

9 You don't like authority. You like to be free to follow your whims and passions, and resent being cooped up. You don't like people knowing what you've been up to.
LOVE PARTNER 193; BUSINESS PARTNER 325

YOUR UNIQUE PERSONALITY READING

Your powers of intuition give your intellect a considerable boost, Birth Number 7. Indeed, you know things even before they are taught to you! The flip side of your keen intellect is that some people find you to be a bit of a know-it-all—or so your Full Name Number of 7 tells us. You know that this is unfair—you just want to share your extensive knowledge. Your Known Name Number reading below can shed more light on the subject.

KNOWN NAME NUMBER

1 You love people—warts, dramas, petty arguments, and all. You could spend all day watching them, charting their progress, laughing at them, and observing them in minute detail.
LOVE PARTNER 114; BUSINESS PARTNER 336

2 Whatever you want to do—do it. Whatever you set your sights on, you will achieve. You have an amazing dedication to your dreams and will work hard to realize your ambitions.
LOVE PARTNER 115; BUSINESS PARTNER 337

3 You have a flair for working with people and functioning as part of a team, and you have a great talent for getting the best out of others. Your persistence is staggering.
LOVE PARTNER 116; BUSINESS PARTNER 338

4 Your word is your bond, and you are prepared to make sacrifices to get the job done. You worry about money quite a bit, and you like to save and provide for the future.
LOVE PARTNER 117; BUSINESS PARTNER 339

5 Always game for a laugh, you are prepared to undertake any challenge, any silly bit of

nonsense, just to be popular and to be the center of attention. You hate being ignored.
LOVE PARTNER 118; BUSINESS PARTNER 331

6 You set your standards, sights, and goals too high. No one will be able to achieve as much as you want and expect to. You worry about so much that you will never sleep peacefully.
LOVE PARTNER 119; BUSINESS PARTNER 332

7 You love a challenge. Give you a difficult task and you spring to life; give you a day off and you sink into depression.
LOVE PARTNER 111; BUSINESS PARTNER 333

8 You work incredibly hard and will achieve great success very young—perhaps too young, because it will spoil you. You will always seek that initial rush of fame and fortune.
LOVE PARTNER 112; BUSINESS PARTNER 334

9 Life will deal you some unpleasant surprises that may take the form of business failures. Will you bounce back? Of course you will, as you have the talent to reinvent yourself.
LOVE PARTNER 113; BUSINESS PARTNER 335

YOUR UNIQUE PERSONALITY READING

Birth number 7, you are a true original: psychic, intuitive, powerful, and influential. These characteristics make you an interesting person, and don't think that others don't see this. People admire your strong character, and your courage in speaking your mind, as we know from your Full Name Number of 8. Your Known Name Number below reveals your inner personality, completing the picture of what you are really all about.

KNOWN NAME NUMBER

1 You have an instinctive understanding of what makes people tick. You are spontaneous and wacky, a little unusual and outlandish, eccentric, and possibly very spiritual.
LOVE PARTNER 124; BUSINESS PARTNER 346

2 You have more energy than the rest of us put together—you are inexhaustible. It would be best if you could find a creative job that would provide a safe outlet for your insanity.
LOVE PARTNER 125; BUSINESS PARTNER 347

3 You are simply crazy, and are great fun to be around. You are always enthusiastic, and are capable of changing directions so quickly that none of us can keep up with you.
LOVE PARTNER 126; BUSINESS PARTNER 348

4 You have moved beyond the normal human range, and have become a sort of mental giant who has lost touch with reality. But you will be successful, wealthy, and well-respected.
LOVE PARTNER 127; BUSINESS PARTNER 349

5 Talented and eccentric, you go around with your head in a book or in the clouds. You

remain cheerfully oblivious to the people around you. You are very bright.
LOVE PARTNER 128; BUSINESS PARTNER 341

6 You can speak very well on your chosen subject—the trouble is we don't understand a single word of it. Do us a favor and try to come down to our level.
LOVE PARTNER 129; BUSINESS PARTNER 342

7 You are very clever, and you want nothing more than to be recognized as an important thinker. You push yourself relentlessly and don't like to take breaks, relax, or unwind.
LOVE PARTNER 121; BUSINESS PARTNER 343

8 You are an independent-minded person with strong views and opinions. You are very bright, and one day you will have all the fame and recognition you so obviously deserve.
LOVE PARTNER 122; BUSINESS PARTNER 344

9 Controversial and larger-than-life, you are not afraid to speak your mind. You are always certain of your facts.
LOVE PARTNER 123; BUSINESS PARTNER 345

BIRTH NUMBER 7
FULL NAME NUMBER 9

Like Sherlock Holmes, you love a good mystery, Known Name Number 9.

YOUR UNIQUE PERSONALITY READING

Sometimes the power you have over others frightens you, Birth Number 7. You know you are psychic, and wonder if it's fair to have such a hold over the unsuspecting minds of others. But there is no need to panic. Others do not see you as manipulative, but rather as a creative, sensitive soul, as we know from your Full Name Number of 9. The full picture of your personality is revealed in your Known Name Number reading below.

KNOWN NAME NUMBER

1 You have a bit of a problem with people who don't work as hard as you or who you think are lazy. You are very practical, and you like nothing better than to get your hands dirty.
LOVE PARTNER 134; BUSINESS PARTNER 356

2 You have the capacity for hard work, persistence, and diligence, and you put these qualities to use in all of your creative endeavors. As a result, you are an excellent entertainer.
LOVE PARTNER 135; BUSINESS PARTNER 357

3 You have quite a reputation for being a perfectionist at work, and you apply yourself industriously to anything you embark upon. You are often seen as a bit of a nonconformist.
LOVE PARTNER 136; BUSINESS PARTNER 358

4 You have a slight problem with authority, and often clash with senior management. However, you are also very good at working from the inside to get things changed.
LOVE PARTNER 137; BUSINESS PARTNER 359

5 You have quite a vision for change, and you stay true to your dreams no matter what

setbacks you encounter. You are idealistic—try to keep your feet on the ground.
LOVE PARTNER 138; BUSINESS PARTNER 351

6 You are inventive and creative, and always at the forefront of new ideas. Revolutionary fervor is something you have by the bucketload.
LOVE PARTNER 139; BUSINESS PARTNER 352

7 You have energy and zeal, and you like to help society. Bless you, but do we really need that much help? I think not, but thank you for trying. You like to express yourself forcefully.
LOVE PARTNER 131; BUSINESS PARTNER 353

8 If there is one thing that gives you great strength, it is your altruistic approach to life—you genuinely care about humanity. Most people have a selfish streak, but you do not.
LOVE PARTNER 132; BUSINESS PARTNER 354

9 You love knowing how things work and often see ways to make them function better. You are cool and detached in love, and prefer research to passion. You are very strange indeed.
LOVE PARTNER 133; BUSINESS PARTNER 355

Lakshmi, the Hindu goddess of wealth and prosperity. Those with a Birth Number of 8 are usually highly determined and tend to acquire great wealth and material success.

YOUR UNIQUE PERSONALITY READING

The number 8 represents willpower and individuality. If this is your Birth Number, you may well be rebellious and unconventional, but you will achieve great wealth and success. Not surprisingly, you appear extremely confident and capable to the outside world, as your Full Name Number of 1 tells us. But there are other sides to you as well—more elusive, but just as interesting. Check your Known Name Number below to uncover these mysteries.

KNOWN NAME NUMBER

1 You are a visionary and an inventor, an innovator and a revolutionary. You have original thoughts and ideas and a creative brain that rarely switches off. Try taking a vacation.
LOVE PARTNER 244; BUSINESS PARTNER 466

2 You are eccentric, rebellious, and ever so slightly mad. You cannot be pigeonholed or summed up. You are as changeable as the sky. Try to be a little more predictable.
LOVE PARTNER 245; BUSINESS PARTNER 467

3 You are creative and talented, and are inclined to be slightly wild at times—but amusingly so. You can be a bit outspoken and may even have a reputation for being difficult.
LOVE PARTNER 246; BUSINESS PARTNER 468

4 You would do anything to get noticed, including behaving like a fool. You like to act up, and can be entertaining. If you are clever, you will translate this behavior into a career.
LOVE PARTNER 247; BUSINESS PARTNER 469

5 You hate being hemmed in or restrained. You despise things being messy, and you have a reputation at work for being a bit of a stickler for punctuality and neatness.
LOVE PARTNER 248; BUSINESS PARTNER 461

6 You like it when people rely on you and would consider it a failure if you ever let them down. You are hardworking, but you also take time off to be with your family.
LOVE PARTNER 249; BUSINESS PARTNER 462

7 You are dependable and reliable. You sound almost boring, and yet you manage to inject humor into everything you do. People like having you around because of your liveliness.
LOVE PARTNER 241; BUSINESS PARTNER 463

8 You know how to work hard, but you also know how to take time out and play. You are popular, successful, friendly, and well-liked.
LOVE PARTNER 242; BUSINESS PARTNER 464

9 You don't like to let people down, and you will move heaven and earth to make sure that you fulfill your obligations. You hate doing menial tasks, and you cannot abide dirt.
LOVE PARTNER 243; BUSINESS PARTNER 465

BIRTH NUMBER

8

FULL NAME NUMBER

2

▲ Brain teasers are your specialty, Known Name Number 2.

YOUR UNIQUE PERSONALITY READING

Ever since you were a child, everyone has always noted your strength of character. Well, Birth Number 8, it's the truth, and you should be proud of it. Stop projecting insecurity, as your Full Name Number 2 shows you are doing—people will not hate you because you are too "together." A better understanding of yourself might help you come across as you really are. Your Known Name Number below can provide the necessary information.

KNOWN NAME NUMBER

1 There is only one word to describe your work output: prodigious. You are extremely hardworking and professional. You can seem a bit intimidating to lesser folk, so be nice to us.
LOVE PARTNER 254; BUSINESS PARTNER 476

2 You are intrigued by logic, mathematics, and puzzles of all sorts. Your clever brain lets you think in three different directions at once. You are also very practical and can fix things.
LOVE PARTNER 255; BUSINESS PARTNER 477

3 You are the research scientist with a heart of gold or the politician with the interest of the people at heart. You may have to wait until you are middle-aged before you gain recognition.
LOVE PARTNER 256; BUSINESS PARTNER 478

4 You have a talent for politics, as you can think quickly on your feet, are intelligent, work well with people, know how to motivate them—and will bend the rules occasionally.
LOVE PARTNER 257; BUSINESS PARTNER 479

5 You are an arch-conservative and a stickler for courtesy and manners. You are polite and

well-spoken, well-educated, and well-read. You are an old-fashioned gentleperson.
LOVE PARTNER 258; BUSINESS PARTNER 471

6 You are prepared to give your all if the cause is right, and you are willing to sacrifice your personal life and relationships to achieve a goal—just so long as the goal isn't too radical.
LOVE PARTNER 259; BUSINESS PARTNER 472

7 You have a talent for putting people at ease and getting them to open up, which serves you well in business. You also work well as a team member. You have atrocious taste in music.
LOVE PARTNER 251; BUSINESS PARTNER 473

8 When you start out after leaving school or university, you may be perceived as a bit clueless and mixed up. If only they knew what a business magnate you are going to become.
LOVE PARTNER 252; BUSINESS PARTNER 474

9 Stop putting work in front of everything else and have some fun. You could also allow others to have their foibles and emotions.
LOVE PARTNER 253; BUSINESS PARTNER 475

YOUR UNIQUE PERSONALITY READING

Those of you with 8 as a Birth Number typically have great organizational skills and are well-respected. People see you as energetic and disciplined—just the type of person to get the job done. Your Full Name Number 3 reveals that others see you as confident. That's why they lay so much responsibility on you. But they don't know all there is to know about you. Your Known Name Number below reveals the inner elements of your personality.

KNOWN NAME NUMBER

1 You like to roll up your sleeves and get on with the job, and you dislike being distracted by anything trivial. If someone is called upon with a sense of responsibility, it will be you.
LOVE PARTNER 264; BUSINESS PARTNER 486

2 You are careful and frugal with money, but are prepared to work hard to earn whatever it is you need to achieve whatever it is you want. You hate being idle, bored, ill, or indulged.
LOVE PARTNER 265; BUSINESS PARTNER 487

3 You can be relied upon in a crisis, and depended upon when the going gets tough. You face up to responsibilities, and always seek excellence in life—and the means to purchase it.
LOVE PARTNER 266; BUSINESS PARTNER 488

4 You are full of stamina, and you can work or party long after the others have fallen by the wayside. You have limitless enthusiasm, and you seem to enjoy life rather too much.
LOVE PARTNER 267; BUSINESS PARTNER 489

5 You have a reputation for being a trifle difficult to work with, as you set high standards. You are blessed with creative talent, but you can be pushy and demanding.
LOVE PARTNER 268; BUSINESS PARTNER 481

6 You are fun to be around, but it is no fun to be on the receiving end of your acerbic sense of humor. You can be cruel and snobbish, but you get away with it because you are charming.
LOVE PARTNER 269; BUSINESS PARTNER 482

7 If there is a solution to be found, you will find it. If there are people to motivate, you will motivate them. You can be outspoken.
LOVE PARTNER 261; BUSINESS PARTNER 483

8 You are kind, with true compassion for others. You aren't money-oriented or ambitious; you are more concerned with finding out how the world works.
LOVE PARTNER 262; BUSINESS PARTNER 484

9 Your interests are wacky and unusual; you love the abnormal and the paranormal. You like to find out new things, and are an avid reader. You are inquisitive about the world.
LOVE PARTNER 263; BUSINESS PARTNER 485

BIRTH NUMBER

8

FULL NAME NUMBER

4

▲ Fine art is a passion of yours, Known Name Number 4.

YOUR UNIQUE PERSONALITY READING

You work well in a team, Birth Number 8, especially when you are leading it. You can push a bit hard, but that is often what it takes to get the job done. Others respond well to your leadership because they see you as reliable—they know that you would do anything for your "troops." That is why they are so faithful to you, Full Name Number 4. But is this confidence in you deserved? Your Known Name Number below can help you find out.

KNOWN NAME NUMBER

1 Sometimes you are just too loud or too much to take, but people are usually pleased to see you. You can be impatient and slipshod at work, but your charm gets you out of trouble.
LOVE PARTNER 274; BUSINESS PARTNER 496

2 By your actions, you inspire us and make us want to be as bright, loud, and exuberant as you. You are optimistic, daring, outspoken, and cheerful. You are awe-inspiring in your bravery.
LOVE PARTNER 275; BUSINESS PARTNER 497

3 You spend all of your time networking, being in the thick of the action, being busy, and being rich. You work hard, but could be more discerning about the jobs you take on.
LOVE PARTNER 276; BUSINESS PARTNER 498

4 You love to travel, collect fine art, and visit museums and art galleries abroad. You are a bit of an optimist in this way—free-thinking and full of new ideas and projects.
LOVE PARTNER 277; BUSINESS PARTNER 499

5 You love fun and the good things in life. You are a kind, sympathetic character who listens to others' problems and tries to help solve them. You like to be surrounded by people.
LOVE PARTNER 278; BUSINESS PARTNER 491

6 You don't like to fail, which can drive you on—even to excess at times. You are clever and use your mind to great advantage. You are successful, practical, and reliable.
LOVE PARTNER 279; BUSINESS PARTNER 492

7 You are unceasingly busy, almost to the point of mania. You simply don't know how to relax or rest, and this can cause stress-related health problems. Take a vacation at once.
LOVE PARTNER 271; BUSINESS PARTNER 493

8 You are quick, decisive, and sharp. No one pulls a fast onc on you, and you love a bargain. You like nothing better than making money out of what other people discard.
LOVE PARTNER 272; BUSINESS PARTNER 494

9 You make a formidable opponent in business deals, and have a ruthless reputation. Try letting others see a softer, gentler side of you.
LOVE PARTNER 273; BUSINESS PARTNER 495

YOUR UNIQUE PERSONALITY READING

You often drive yourself—and others—crazy with your quest for perfection. You can't help it though; perfectionism is a common trait for Birth Number 8. Lucky for you, people see you as charming, witty, and fun to be around, as we know from your Full Name Number of 5. But this is not the whole story. There is so much more to you. Check your Known Name Number below. You may be surprised at what you find out.

KNOWN NAME NUMBER

1 You are up before anyone else, and are out buying and selling while others are lingering over breakfast. And when others go home for the day, you are still wheeling and dealing.
LOVE PARTNER 284; BUSINESS PARTNER 416

2 You have an easygoing attitude, and are very easy to get along with—even if it is all a sham. You don't particularly like to work with your hands, as you are a thinker—or schemer.
LOVE PARTNER 285; BUSINESS PARTNER 417

3 You aren't a great one for relaxing, and anything you do to wind down usually involves some element of work. You like to be busy, but must learn to switch off occasionally.
LOVE PARTNER 286; BUSINESS PARTNER 418

4 Some people think you are sleepy and slow; others think you stubborn. Neither of these perceptions are true, of course. The truth about you is much deeper than that, as you well know.
LOVE PARTNER 287; BUSINESS PARTNER 419

5 You are a curious anomaly in this modern world—someone who actually cares about old-fashioned values. Values are what you are all about, but they may hold you back.
LOVE PARTNER 288; BUSINESS PARTNER 411

6 Everything seems to move too fast, too furiously, for you these days. You prefer calm and peacefulness, order and routine. You are a sentimental romantic from a bygone age.
LOVE PARTNER 289; BUSINESS PARTNER 412

7 You are a worrier by nature. You worry that the world has gone to the dogs and that no one does a good job any more. You worry about what the future will bring for your children.
LOVE PARTNER 281; BUSINESS PARTNER 413

8 You believe in order, ritual, and tradition, and don't take to new ideas very quickly. You are the strong, silent type who keeps to yourself. Few people can read your thoughts.
LOVE PARTNER 282; BUSINESS PARTNER 414

9 You are a loyal friend, and you pay attention to duty. You are a true friend in a time of crisis. But if someone crosses you, watch out.
LOVE PARTNER 283; BUSINESS PARTNER 415

BIRTH NUMBER

8

6

FULL NAME NUMBER

YOUR UNIQUE PERSONALITY READING

If your Birth Number is 8, chances are you are not afraid to speak your mind, and you don't care if your opinion is unpopular. This often comes as a surprise to those who don't know you very well. Many of your acquaintances see you as lighthearted, as we know from your Full Name Number of 6. They have no idea that such conviction lurks behind that carefree exterior. Your Known Name Number below reveals another side to you.

KNOWN NAME NUMBER

1 You are excellent at organizing things—anything from a children's party to a pop concert. You are an honest person and wouldn't know how to lie—even if you wanted to.
LOVE PARTNER 294; BUSINESS PARTNER 426

2 You are a hardworking person who shuns the limelight and prefers to work backstage. Without you, the show simply couldn't go on. You give everyone else the credit.
LOVE PARTNER 295; BUSINESS PARTNER 427

3 You are good with people, and you are tolerant and patient. You set high standards and don't take kindly to sloth or dishonesty in the workplace. You are a stickler for rules.
LOVE PARTNER 296; BUSINESS PARTNER 428

4 You don't really know how to relax, do you? You work until you drop and then complain about exhaustion. When you do take time off, you occupy your time gardening or socializing.
LOVE PARTNER 297; BUSINESS PARTNER 429

5 Anyone falling in love with you will get a high return on their investment, as you give your whole heart and soul to the relationship. You are a true romantic.
LOVE PARTNER 298; BUSINESS PARTNER 421

6 You have great strength of body and character, and were born to lead, even if no one is following yet. There is virtually no subject that you cannot talk about intelligently.
LOVE PARTNER 299; BUSINESS PARTNER 422

7 Life for you would be boring if you weren't always planning the next great adventure. You are one of life's motivators, and the planet would be dull without you around.
LOVE PARTNER 291; BUSINESS PARTNER 423

8 You are brave and reckless on the outside, having courage in abundance. But in your head, you often feel lonely and unloved. Start reaching out more to others.
LOVE PARTNER 292; BUSINESS PARTNER 424

9 You make rash decisions at times, and are forced to live with the consequences. Luckily you will mellow as you grow older.
LOVE PARTNER 293; BUSINESS PARTNER 425

BIRTH NUMBER **8**

FULL NAME NUMBER **7**

▲ You seek the scales of justice, Known Name Number 7.

YOUR UNIQUE PERSONALITY READING

When put in a group situation, you always wind up taking control. Well, why not? You're good at leading others, right Birth Number 8? Just beware of the image that you project to others. Although they respect you, they sometimes find you frighteningly cold, or so your Full Name Number of 7 tells us. Maybe you can find a happy medium after all. Check your Known Name Number reading below for a sense of what you're really capable of.

KNOWN NAME NUMBER

1 You have many friends who think the world of you, even if you exhaust them. You do like to be in charge, though, and should give your friends a little more say in how you socialize.
LOVE PARTNER 214; BUSINESS PARTNER 436

2 You like to take risks, so you will not be successful at any job in which you feel trapped. Be an explorer and you'll go far, but you may suffer setbacks due to your nature.
LOVE PARTNER 215; BUSINESS PARTNER 437

3 You don't really have any leisure time, as you're always so busy doing other things. The way you relax may seem like hard work to the rest of us, but you enjoy being active.
LOVE PARTNER 216; BUSINESS PARTNER 438

4 You feel best when you are in love. You give everything in love and feel hurt if let down. You do lose interest easily, however, and like to move on. You can be unconventional at times.
LOVE PARTNER 217; BUSINESS PARTNER 439

5 You have enormous energy for love, and your intensity can wear out a lesser soul. You are affectionate, caring, and loving, and you simply glow when you are loved in return.
LOVE PARTNER 218; BUSINESS PARTNER 431

6 You have limitless energy and boundless enthusiasm. What more could anyone want? Perhaps a bit of gentleness now and again. You are very trustworthy, and can be relied upon.
LOVE PARTNER 219; BUSINESS PARTNER 432

7 You just pretend to be crazy, so that people will tell you more than they should. You're good at getting information out of people. You would make a good lawyer.
LOVE PARTNER 211; BUSINESS PARTNER 433

8 You are quick and sharp-witted but also unpredictable. No one knows how they stand with you. You can be very intense.
LOVE PARTNER 212; BUSINESS PARTNER 434

9 You are a loner, although one can always find you surrounded by crowds of people. You are adept at handling tricky situations. You are capable, controlled, in charge, and up front.
LOVE PARTNER 213; BUSINESS PARTNER 435

BIRTH NUMBER 8

FULL NAME NUMBER 8

▲ Like Benjamin Franklin, you are a born inventor, Known Name Number 1.

YOUR UNIQUE PERSONALITY READING

Ever since you were a child, you have always had a rebellious streak in you, Birth Number 8. Now that you are an adult, your chutzpah is paying off in the business world, and you are proud of yourself. Other people recognize you as a leader and innovator—as your Full Name Number 8 tells us—which is why you are so successful. But are you as perfect as you seem? Your Known Name Number reading below can help you answer this question.

KNOWN NAME NUMBER

1 Your work is important to you. You are so bright and clever that if you aren't employed using your brains, you are being wasted. You are a researcher, an inventor, and a mad scientist.
LOVE PARTNER 224; BUSINESS PARTNER 446

2 You have a unique way of thinking that allows you to make quantum leaps of logic that we mere mortals can only dream of. You are one of the great lateral thinkers of this world.
LOVE PARTNER 225; BUSINESS PARTNER 447

3 You have a quirky sense of humor, and people often raise their eyebrows at how coarse you can be. This is incongruous with your other refinements and your love of good taste.
LOVE PARTNER 226; BUSINESS PARTNER 448

4 You are a private person, and your partner may complain that he or she never really knows where they stand with you. Perhaps you should open up a bit and share your feelings.
LOVE PARTNER 227; BUSINESS PARTNER 449

5 You are larger than life, twice as grand as anybody else, twice as fabulous and ten times more superb. But I don't know why I am telling you all this—you already know it.
LOVE PARTNER 228; BUSINESS PARTNER 441

6 You are one of those people that others turn to for advice and information. People value what you have to say, and regard it as a great honor when you share your views with them.
LOVE PARTNER 229; BUSINESS PARTNER 442

7 You hate being bored, poor, or lied to— and why not, for you are important and irreplaceable. The world would be a duller place without you to inspire the rest of us.
LOVE PARTNER 221; BUSINESS PARTNER 443

8 You don't really like work, do you? You like the status, the money, and the kudos—but the actual work? Not your cup of tea.
LOVE PARTNER 222; BUSINESS PARTNER 444

9 You have such a natural air of authority about you that you get elevated to positions of power without really having to do anything. You are a born leader of the boardroom.
LOVE PARTNER 223; BUSINESS PARTNER 445

BIRTH NUMBER **8**

FULL NAME NUMBER **9**

YOUR UNIQUE PERSONALITY READING

When something needs doing, you hunker down and do it. That's what's so great about you, Birth Number 8, and it's a trait that others admire. You may not know this, but people also respect your courage in always sticking up for the underdogs of this world; we know this from your Full Name Number of 9. What else do you have to offer this world? Quite a bit. Your Known Name Number below reveals more about your inner personality.

KNOWN NAME NUMBER

1 Your character is deep and unfathomable— at least that's what most people think. But, in reality, you are very easy to understand and know. If only people wouldn't be so hasty.
LOVE PARTNER 234; BUSINESS PARTNER 456

2 You can be charming and debonair, sophisticated and elegant. You can also be ruthless and cruel, manipulative and calculating. You can be many things. Which is the real you?
LOVE PARTNER 235; BUSINESS PARTNER 457

3 For you, the means always justify the end. If a problem needs solving, you solve it. However, sometimes you may sail a little close to the wind when it comes to finding solutions.
LOVE PARTNER 235; BUSINESS PARTNER 457

4 You are romantic and sensuous, and you have a subtle sense of humor. You love being surrounded by admirers and having the world wait on your next word.
LOVE PARTNER 237; BUSINESS PARTNER 459

5 You are a kind, sympathetic character who listens well to others' problems—you even do your best to help solve them. You like to be surrounded by people, and are well-loved.
LOVE PARTNER 238; BUSINESS PARTNER 451

6 You have a wonderful sense of humor, although it can be a little teasing at times. You are loving and caring. You are good with your hands, and you are creative and practical.
LOVE PARTNER 239; BUSINESS PARTNER 452

7 You are a born gossip but also a good friend. Some of your friends would be touched to realize how much you care about them.
LOVE PARTNER 231; BUSINESS PARTNER 453

8 You are attractive and vivacious, although you feign humility about your good looks. You don't compromise, and you hold very strong views about how the world should be.
LOVE PARTNER 232; BUSINESS PARTNER 454

9 You set an example for us all. You are loyal and trustworthy, friendly and enterprising, cheerful and sincere. You probably don't realize what an inspiration you are—or maybe you do.
LOVE PARTNER 233; BUSINESS PARTNER 455

BIRTH NUMBER
9

FULL NAME NUMBER
1

◀ A depiction of Apollo playing the cithara on 4th-century BC vase. People with a Birth Number of 9 are usually expressive and enjoy artistic pursuits such as music, painting, and writing.

YOUR UNIQUE PERSONALITY READING

If your Birth Number is 9, you are probably a very expressive person. This expression can take a number of forms: painting, writing, composing music—all of these activities make you happy. Some people find you intimidating and exhausting, according to your Full Name Number of 1. But you are infinitely more complex than this. Check your Known Name Number reading below; you may want to bring your inner personality to the fore.

KNOWN NAME NUMBER

1 You have never learned the meaning of the word "can't." You simply do. You are a true pragmatist. You aren't wacky or unconventional, which means you get the job done.
LOVE PARTNER 344; BUSINESS PARTNER 566

2 You are resourceful and versatile, and are able to turn your hand to pretty well anything you choose. You like to stay on the right side of the law.
LOVE PARTNER 345; BUSINESS PARTNER 567

3 You are independent with a mind of your own, and you are always willing to share your opinions. If there's one thing you are renowned for, it's your talkative nature.
LOVE PARTNER 346; BUSINESS PARTNER 568

4 You are a kind person who cares about those around you, but you don't care too much about world politics—all that matters to you is that your loved ones are well fed and happy.
LOVE PARTNER 347; BUSINESS PARTNER 59

5 You can do anything that requires talking and thinking fast on your feet. You don't like routine, and are best suited to jobs in which you have the freedom to move around.
LOVE PARTNER 348; BUSINESS PARTNER 561

6 The key word for you is communication. You may not be a brilliant ideas person, but you can certainly convey ideas to other people, even if the ideas are not your own.
LOVE PARTNER 349; BUSINESS PARTNER 562

7 You may be regarded as manipulative, but that's only because you are so quick to see how a situation can benefit you. If the rest of us are too slow, then who can blame you?
LOVE PARTNER 341; BUSINESS PARTNER 563

8 You like to break the rules. This can get you into trouble, but you usually talk your way out of it. You are a risk-taker, and sometimes lie through your teeth to get what you want.
LOVE PARTNER 342; BUSINESS PARTNER 564

9 People may accuse you of having no depth, but that's not really the case. It's just that on the surface you seem so carefree.
LOVE PARTNER 343; BUSINESS PARTNER 565

△ You always offer comfort to those in distress, Known Name Number 7.

YOUR UNIQUE PERSONALITY READING

You are a poet at heart, Birth Number 9. Creative and imaginative, if you could spend all of your time exploring the depths of the human soul, you would. On the outside, you get along well with people, and are caring and supportive—at least according to your Full Name Number of 2. But I'm sure you know there is more to you than meets the eye. In your Known Name Number reading below you will find your inner personality revealed.

KNOWN NAME NUMBER

1 You are known for your honesty and quick wit. You are a capable, practical sort of person who can fix things, make things, and generally be useful. You like your independence.
LOVE PARTNER 354; BUSINESS PARTNER 576

2 You don't stay still for very long. You need a job that gives you a lot of independence and trust, because you hate having anyone breathing down your neck or looking over your shoulder.
LOVE PARTNER 355; BUSINESS PARTNER 577

3 You love being refined and well-to-do, and take pride in your personal appearance. You want to be somebody. You have lofty ambitions, and you work hard to achieve them.
LOVE PARTNER 356; BUSINESS PARTNER 578

4 You are intelligent and have an eye for detail. You take care about your appearance, and some might say you're a bit of a dandy. You are popular and are appreciated by your friends.
LOVE PARTNER 357; BUSINESS PARTNER 579

5 You are ambitious, but don't like taking orders; you'd better climb the ladder as

quickly as possible, so you won't have to. The trouble is, you are also supremely lazy.
LOVE PARTNER 358; BUSINESS PARTNER 571

6 You want your needs to be attended to immediately. You can be a little egocentric, but you are enthusiastic, trustworthy, and loving.
LOVE PARTNER 359; BUSINESS PARTNER 572

7 If someone needs a friend, you are there. If someone needs a shoulder to cry on, it's probably your shoulder they choose. You're a loyal, faithful companion.
LOVE PARTNER 351; BUSINESS PARTNER 573

8 You are incredibly idealistic. You hate conflict and confrontation, although you can cope with them if they arise. Some people see you as self-righteous.
LOVE PARTNER 352; BUSINESS PARTNER 574

9 You have an enormous heart, and care so deeply about things that you spend a lot of time in tears. You are also ambitious, and have a gift for seeing into other people's souls.
LOVE PARTNER 353; BUSINESS PARTNER 575

PERSONALITY GUIDE

YOUR UNIQUE PERSONALITY READING

What a great champion of the underdog you are, Birth Number 9! Congratulations. Standing up for the rights of others takes courage and conviction, both of which you have in abundance. You come off as very sure of yourself, according to your Full Name Number of 3, which helps you in your quest to convince others to join you in your crusades. Your Known Name Number reading below casts some light on your enigmatic inner persona.

KNOWN NAME NUMBER

1 We know you like your independence, so what's the problem? We also know you are headstrong, and have no wish to curb your freedom. Stop being so argumentative.
LOVE PARTNER 364; BUSINESS PARTNER 586

2 For some of us, this life is just a learning experience. For you, it is purely fun. This is a life off for you, and you can coast as much as you want without concern. Enjoy your freedom.
LOVE PARTNER 365; BUSINESS PARTNER 587

3 You like being busy and active—but is all this a front to stop you from thinking? You will have to face your inner demons one day; better to get it over with. You have the courage.
LOVE PARTNER 366; BUSINESS PARTNER 588

4 If you are not a politician, then what are you wasting your time on? You have a caring side that needs an outlet, and politics will use your considerable communication skills.
LOVE PARTNER 367; BUSINESS PARTNER 589

5 What a charmer you are. You love socializing and have no problem with using your friends for business deals and money-making ventures. Luckily, they trust you.
LOVE PARTNER 368; BUSINESS PARTNER 581

6 You are quick and lively. You love looking for opportunities, especially to increase your wealth. You don't like to admit that you have emotions, let alone show them.
LOVE PARTNER 369; BUSINESS PARTNER 582

7 You certainly have a way with the opposite sex. You can seduce pretty well anyone you take a liking to—and, by golly, there are quite a few of those around at any time.
LOVE PARTNER 361; BUSINESS PARTNER 583

8 You have a good memory. You pick up skills quickly, possess a sharp intelligence, and can make decisions with great speed and confidence.
LOVE PARTNER 362; BUSINESS PARTNER 584

9 You find it easy to talk to people. They, in turn, are drawn to your personality and charm. Your friends find you witty, amusing, and lots of fun to be with and to have around.
LOVE PARTNER 363; BUSINESS PARTNER 585

BIRTH NUMBER

9

FULL NAME NUMBER

4

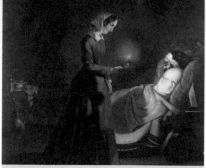

▲ Like Florence Nightingale, you have a caring nature, Known Name Number 8.

YOUR UNIQUE PERSONALITY READING

Those with a Birth Number of 9 find themselves drawn to the exotic, even freakish, elements of life. They are what makes life worth living, right? Isn't it funny then that despite the strange company you keep, people would still describe you as down-to-earth—the practical, reliable type, as we know from your Full Name Number of 4. Why this dichotomy? Perhaps your Known Name Number reading below can shed some light on this.

KNOWN NAME NUMBER

1 You love socializing and would drop anything to go partying. You adore being around people. You love work, so long as you can network. You are a bit of a name-dropper.
LOVE PARTNER 374; BUSINESS PARTNER 596

2 Work is important to you, and it is where your critical side can be used to great effect. You have an eye for detail and like to see a job through. You should learn to relax a bit.
LOVE PARTNER 375; BUSINESS PARTNER 597

3 You are good at solving problems and would make a good engineer. You would also make a good money manager, although you might not be effective at managing your own.
LOVE PARTNER 376; BUSINESS PARTNER 598

4 When you apply yourself at work, you succeed. Your ambitions will be fulfilled, just so long as you don't clash with the boss. You cannot work for anyone you think foolish.
LOVE PARTNER 377; BUSINESS PARTNER 599

5 If you allow anyone to get close to you, then they become friends for life. The trouble is that the harsh façade you put up, combined with your critical nature, can put people off.
LOVE PARTNER 378; BUSINESS PARTNER 591

6 This outspoken front you put up is just that—a front. If you decide to drop it, you are warm and friendly, supportive and loyal, kind and generous, and a trusty friend.
LOVE PARTNER 379; BUSINESS PARTNER 592

7 You are just too easygoing to devote time and energy to work, and you prefer to socialize and shop. Some people might think you are shallow and spoiled, but you don't care.
LOVE PARTNER 371; BUSINESS PARTNER 593

8 If you devote yourself to either an artistic career or one where you care for others, you will do well. Avoid finance and corporate life.
LOVE PARTNER 372; BUSINESS PARTNER 594

9 You can work alone, but you are much better off working in a team. You need to be around other people; when left alone, you tend to become extremely dreamy and unrealistic.
LOVE PARTNER 373; BUSINESS PARTNER 595

BIRTH NUMBER **9**

FULL NAME NUMBER **5**

YOUR UNIQUE PERSONALITY READING

You can be belligerent at times—a typical characteristic of a Birth Number 9—but you do your best to rein in this aspect of your personality. You also have a great deal going for you: you are a creative, imaginative soul. Others like having you around, as we know from your Full Name Number of 5, so long as you don't get too confrontational. Perhaps a clue to controlling your temper lies in your Known Name Number reading below.

KNOWN NAME NUMBER

1 You have a reputation for being a leader, but you've never actually looked back over your shoulder to see if anyone is following. Look back now and you may see no one.
LOVE PARTNER 384; BUSINESS PARTNER 516

2 You are a good listener, and any advice that you give is accepted as sound and practical. You have a unique talent for making new friends easily and readily, and you enjoy socializing.
LOVE PARTNER 385; BUSINESS PARTNER 517

3 You may well be a trail-blazer, a trendsetter, a pioneer—but a leader? No, not really. You may have people following you, but that's their business. You just go your own way.
LOVE PARTNER 386; BUSINESS PARTNER 518

4 You are very quick-thinking and you have a lively brain that needs to be stimulated. You have the capacity for several careers in your life, and you rarely get stuck in a rut.
LOVE PARTNER 387; BUSINESS PARTNER 519

5 Earning money for its own sake doesn't interest you, but having enough to purchase excitement and prestige does. You have a knack for making—and losing—a small fortune.
LOVE PARTNER 388; BUSINESS PARTNER 511

6 You have a wide circle of friends and your taste in them is broad and varied. You love entertaining, although there are times when you need to shut the door and see no one for a while.
LOVE PARTNER 389; BUSINESS PARTNER 512

7 It is only within the structure and intimacy of a relationship that you thrive and shine. It's as if you have to have someone to care about or all that energy is worthless.
LOVE PARTNER 381; BUSINESS PARTNER 513

8 Just wait a little while longer and the world will be ready to accept your ideas. Don't push. Don't argue. It's just a question of time.
LOVE PARTNER 382; BUSINESS PARTNER 514

9 Niagara in a barrel holds no fear for you; nor does climbing mountains or canoeing the Amazon. You have more courage than is needed in this modern world.
LOVE PARTNER 383; BUSINESS PARTNER 515

YOUR UNIQUE PERSONALITY READING

Always hanging around with the wild crowd, aren't you, Birth Number 9? You befriend all sorts of odd characters—these are the kinds of people that make you tick. To an outsider, you seem to prefer the company of your family—or at least this is what a Full Name Number of 6 reveals. It may be time to air some other aspects of your personality. Your Known Name Number reading below may show you which parts of yourself to reveal.

KNOWN NAME NUMBER

1 You cannot fail to succeed, as you have more ideas in one day than we have in a lifetime. You will translate some of them into a successful business and will be very wealthy one day.
LOVE PARTNER 394; BUSINESS PARTNER 526

2 By being as eccentric as you are, you only draw attention to the unconventional aspects of your ideas. If you were to blend in more, you would go much farther.
LOVE PARTNER 395; BUSINESS PARTNER 527

3 You are relentless in your pursuit of your dreams, and will continue planning and scheming long after others have given up. You are very resourceful and determined.
LOVE PARTNER 396; BUSINESS PARTNER 528

4 There is nothing you hate more than being bored, and so you keep yourself busy with new projects. You hate to be kept waiting, and are capable of holding a grudge for a long time.
LOVE PARTNER 397; BUSINESS PARTNER 529

5 You are always at the forefront of a new project. You will do well in any occupation in which your innovative spirit is allowed to flourish, but badly if you feel stifled and bored.
LOVE PARTNER 398; BUSINESS PARTNER 521

6 You are creative, with strong ideas that cry out for expression. You hate rules and find it difficult to be supervised. If running your own creative business, you will thrive.
LOVE PARTNER 399; BUSINESS PARTNER 522

7 It is important that you feel relaxed and comfortable at work, as your environment is very important to you. You are unconventional and can be trusted to work unsupervised.
LOVE PARTNER 391; BUSINESS PARTNER 523

8 You are able to hide your emotions well when hurt, and it takes you a long time to get over a failed relationship. You have a big, soft heart, and you deserve better than you've had.
LOVE PARTNER 392; BUSINESS PARTNER 524

9 Socializing is what life is all about for you. You like to have people around you, but you never take to them as much as they take to you.
LOVE PARTNER 393; BUSINESS PARTNER 525

BIRTH NUMBER 9

FULL NAME NUMBER 7

▲ Spiritual well-being is very important to you, Known Name Number 7.

YOUR UNIQUE PERSONALITY READING

You of the Birth Number 9 can be complex creatures: expressive and poetic one minute, and then quarrelsome the next. Regardless of this duality, people constantly seek your opinion, as your Full Name Number 7 tells us. Your reputation as an intellectual always precedes you. But you are even more of an enigma than you initially appear. Your Known Name Number reading below provides another piece to the puzzle that is the real you.

KNOWN NAME NUMBER

1 Nothing really sustains your interest for long, and you may well need at least two jobs to keep you focused. You're not motivated by money, so financial rewards are not a lure.
LOVE PARTNER 314; BUSINESS PARTNER 536

2 You have a talent for being in the right place at the right time. Trust your instincts and you can't go wrong. You are extremely inventive, and can build just about anything.
LOVE PARTNER 315; BUSINESS PARTNER 537

3 As you have immense charm, it's probably best if you employ others rather than be an employee yourself. You work most effectively in the face of tight deadlines and crises.
LOVE PARTNER 316; BUSINESS PARTNER 538

4 You are one of life's great leaders, always in the thick of things. Self-confidence is not a problem for you, and you find it easy to draw attention to yourself.
LOVE PARTNER 317; BUSINESS PARTNER 539

5 Your perception of your own importance makes you seem a little smug at times, and this offends some people. Tone down your ego a bit and you will be better liked.
LOVE PARTNER 318; BUSINESS PARTNER 531

6 Nothing is more satisfying to you than closing a business deal. Being alone frightens you, and you constantly seek the company of friends. You are very reliable in a crisis.
LOVE PARTNER 319; BUSINESS PARTNER 532

7 You are a loving, creative person and are jealous of no one. You are slow to anger and tend not to jump to conclusions. You are very spiritual and a kind person.
LOVE PARTNER 311; BUSINESS PARTNER 533

8 People gather around you constantly; but you tire of them quickly, and replace them as soon as they become predictable. Relaxation is difficult for you; you always have a project going.
LOVE PARTNER 312; BUSINESS PARTNER 534

9 You are easily bored, and love starting new undertakings. You hate to be kept waiting, and can be quarrelsome when tired or restless.
LOVE PARTNER 313; BUSINESS PARTNER 535

BIRTH NUMBER

9

8

FULL NAME NUMBER

▲ Your boundless energy needs an outlet, Known Name Number 7.

YOUR UNIQUE PERSONALITY READING

It is often hard for people with the Birth Number 9 to find a mate. This difficulty stems from the fact that you can be, well, difficult. Much of your irascibility stems from the feeling that nobody really understands you. Others see you as unconventional, as we know from your Full Name Number of 8, and this might also scare potential partners away. Take a look at your Known Name Number below for a better understanding of yourself.

KNOWN NAME NUMBER

1 You don't just feel things, you experience them with every fiber of your being. When others are merely sad, you are totally distraught; when others are happy, you are elated.
LOVE PARTNER 324; BUSINESS PARTNER 546

2 You are intelligent and responsive. Because you feel things so intensely, you have a wealth of experience that others can only guess at. You are artistic and a bit enigmatic.
LOVE PARTNER 325; BUSINESS PARTNER 547

3 If you learn to control your passion, you can achieve success in any field. If you don't, you will end up crazy and eccentric. You have great talent and an urgent need to express it.
LOVE PARTNER 326; BUSINESS PARTNER 548

4 Due to your powerful emotions, you can sometimes be rash in your choice of partner. What you see, you instantly want. Learn to want what you need and not the other way around.
LOVE PARTNER 327; BUSINESS PARTNER 549

5 You set very high standards in your own life, and expect order and harmony around you.

You dislike having that order upset and are not very good at adapting to change.
LOVE PARTNER 328; BUSINESS PARTNER 541

6 You are a wild child, with great artistic expression and a dislike of the humdrum. You hate gossip, being bored, being bossed around, being doubted, and being teased.
LOVE PARTNER 329; BUSINESS PARTNER 542

7 You have great enthusiasm—sometimes too much for the people around you—but you're never bored or depressed. You love sports.
LOVE PARTNER 321; BUSINESS PARTNER 543

8 What a contrary soul you are. On the surface, you're calm and responsible, but underneath lurks passion and mischief. You can be stubborn, even if you know you are wrong.
LOVE PARTNER 322; BUSINESS PARTNER 544

9 Outwardly, you are calm and organized, but underneath lurks a simmering cauldron of repressed passions and desires. Only your closest lovers will ever know the real you.
LOVE PARTNER 323; BUSINESS PARTNER 545

YOUR UNIQUE PERSONALITY READING

Both your Birth and Full Name Numbers are 9, which means that everyone recognizes you for the expressive, creative individual you are. They especially admire the way you stand up for the downtrodden. Danger and excitement attract you, and you are never dull to be around. But you don't always have to play the part of the quirky friend, you know. Your Known Name Number reading below illuminates other parts of your personality.

KNOWN NAME NUMBER

1 You will get to the very top, but only because those around you are prepared to sacrifice it all for you. That is a great responsibility. I wonder if you take it as seriously as you should?
LOVE PARTNER 334; BUSINESS PARTNER 556

2 The big picture is always clear to you, and you delegate easily. You tend to farm out the most difficult parts of the work to others; but, then, what's wrong with that?
LOVE PARTNER 335; BUSINESS PARTNER 557

3 Trust you to get the job done, both within budget and on time. Listen to your heart and you may become more successful in your career. Dare to dream it—and then dare to do it.
LOVE PARTNER 336; BUSINESS PARTNER 558

4 You fool a lot of people who may think you a lightweight until they get to know you. You hate being let down, but you recover fast. You dislike others seeing you upset.
LOVE PARTNER 337; BUSINESS PARTNER 559

5 You are a loner who enjoys solitude and your own company, but you are friendly and well-liked by others. You are a little circumspect of love and relationships.
LOVE PARTNER 338; BUSINESS PARTNER 551

6 You are highly unpredictable, but sometimes behave with such normalcy that we are fooled into thinking that you've become one of us. What a tricky one you are.
LOVE PARTNER 339; BUSINESS PARTNER 552

7 Most people would describe you as eccentric. This does not always inspire confidence in business. If you could blend in a bit more, you would make more headway.
LOVE PARTNER 331; BUSINESS PARTNER 553

8 You are so determined to be right that it never enters your head to lie or to back off. You can be very pigheaded and will never admit that you are wrong. And why should you?
LOVE PARTNER 332; BUSINESS PARTNER 554

9 You are enigmatic, full of wonder and secrets. You are a child of the universe and not a mortal at all. What are you doing here?
LOVE PARTNER 333; BUSINESS PARTNER 555

INDEX

CREDITS

Quantum Books would like to acknowledge the following for supplying images reproduced in this book:

Alamy: pp.7, 20, 132 The Art Archive; p.36 Interfoto; p.49 (below left) World History Archive; p.92 Chronicle; p.122 Louise Batalla Duran

British Library: pp.15, 34, 57, 62, 71, 87, 91, 96, 99, 117, 124 (www.flickr.com/photos/britishlibrary)

Corbis: p.32 Christie's Images; p.52 Stefano Bianchetti

Getty Images: p.13 Photo12/UIG; p.41 DeAgostini; p.72 CSA Images

Library of Congress: pp.21, 121, 126

Shutterstock: p.2 Zarya Maxim Alexandrovich; p.5 (number strips used throughout) Login; pp.5 (circles), 50–51 adike; pp.9, 25, 31, 64, 75, 82, 89, 101 Everett Collection; pp.10-11 marekuliasz; p.12 (no.1) Olga1992; p.12 (no.2) Kapreski; p.12 (no.3) ProStockStudio; p.12 (no.4) Vector Draco; p.12 (nos.5, 6) Deliza; p.12 (no.7) ashva; p.12 (no.8) emerge; p.12 (no.9) Voropaev Vasiliy; p.18 Oleg Golovnev; p.24 Nancy Bauer; p.27 Bavorndej; p.39 (nos.1, 3, 4, 5, 6, 8) cajoer; p.39 (no.9) VoodooDot; p.47 (below right) Yurumi; p.48 (below right) Digital N; p.49 (below right) Anielius; p.58 Wildnerdpix; p.61 Sergey Nivens; p.67 Belight; p.68 Catherine Glazkova; p.76 Yuliya Evstratenko; p.78 Malchev; p.84 Creativa Images; pp.95, 109 Marzolino; pp.104, 114, 130 Everett Historical; p.118 Dao Xuan Cu; p.139 Vinogradov Illya; p.140 Photobac

Wellcome Library, London: pp.6, 8, 17, 19, 22, 29, 30, 38, 42, 54, 80, 102, 106, 129, 134, 136 (www.creativecommons.org/licenses/by/4.0)

While every effort has been made to credit contributors, Quantum Books would like to apologize should there have been any omissions or errors and would be pleased to make the appropriate correction to future editions of the book.